Frank Richard Stockton

A Chosen Few

Short Stories

Frank Richard Stockton

A Chosen Few
Short Stories

ISBN/EAN: 9783744704748

Printed in Europe, USA, Canada, Australia, Japan

Cover: Foto ©Thomas Meinert / pixelio.de

More available books at **www.hansebooks.com**

A CHOSEN FEW

CAMEO EDITION.

♣

♣

Each, one volume, 16mo.
Half Calf, g. t., $2.75; half levant, $3.50; cloth, $1.25

A CHOSEN FEW

SHORT STORIES

BY

FRANK R. STOCKTON

WITH AN ETCHED PORTRAIT BY W. H. W. BICKNELL

NEW YORK

CHARLES SCRIBNER'S SONS

1895

PREFACE

THE stories contained in this little volume were chosen, by virtue of a sort of literary civil-service examination, in order that they might be grouped together as a representative class of the author's best-known work in this line.

Several of these stories have points of peculiar interest to the author. For instance, "Negative Gravity" was composed in Switzerland when the author was temporarily confined to the house in full view of unreachable Alps.

"His Wife's Deceased Sister" was suggested by an editorial disposition to compare all the author's work with one previous production, and to discard everything which did not accord exactly with the particular story which had been selected as a standard of merit.

"The Lady, or the Tiger?" was printed in the

hope that the author might receive the cheerful coöperation of some of his readers in a satisfactory solution of the problem contained in the little story; but although he has had much valuable assistance in this direction he has also been the recipient of a great deal of scolding.

After reading several stories by Clark Russell, the author's mind was led to consider the possibility of inventing some sort of shipwreck which had never yet been made the subject of a story. His efforts in this line resulted in " The Remarkable Wreck of the ' Thomas Hyke.' "

" A Piece of Red Calico " is a description, with exaggerated points, of an actual experience.

CONTENTS

A TALE OF NEGATIVE GRAVITY

A TALE OF NEGATIVE GRAVITY

Y wife and I were staying at a small town in northern Italy; and on a certain pleasant afternoon in spring we had taken a walk of six or seven miles to see the sun set behind some low mountains to the west of the town. Most of our walk had been along a hard, smooth highway, and then we turned into a series of narrower roads, sometimes bordered by walls, and sometimes by light fences of reed or cane. Nearing the mountain, to a low spur of which we intended to ascend, we easily scaled a wall about four feet high, and found ourselves upon pasture-land, which led, sometimes by gradual ascents, and sometimes by bits of rough climbing, to the spot we wished to reach. We were afraid we were a little late, and therefore hurried on, running up the grassy hills, and bounding briskly over the rough and rocky places. I carried a knapsack strapped firmly to my shoulders,

and under my wife's arm was a large, soft basket
of a kind much used by tourists. Her arm was
passed through the handles and around the bottom
of the basket, which she pressed closely to her
side. This was the way she always carried it.
The basket contained two bottles of wine, one
sweet for my wife, and another a little acid for
myself. Sweet wines give me a headache.

When we reached the grassy bluff, well known
thereabouts to lovers of sunset views, I stepped
immediately to the edge to gaze upon the scene,
but my wife sat down to take a sip of wine, for
she was very thirsty; and then, leaving her basket,
she came to my side. The scene was indeed one
of great beauty. Beneath us stretched a wide
valley of many shades of green, with a little river
running through it, and red-tiled houses here and
there. Beyond rose a range of mountains, pink,
pale green, and purple where their tips caught the
reflection of the setting sun, and of a rich gray-
green in shadows. Beyond all was the blue Italian
sky, illumined by an especially fine sunset.

My wife and I are Americans, and at the time
of this story were middle-aged people and very
fond of seeing in each other's company whatever
there was of interest or beauty around us. We
had a son about twenty-two years old, of whom
we were also very fond; but he was not with us,
being at that time a student in Germany. Although
we had good health, we were not very robust peo-

ple, and, under ordinary circumstances, not much given to long country tramps. I was of medium size, without much muscular development, while my wife was quite stout, and growing stouter.

The reader may, perhaps, be somewhat surprised that a middle-aged couple, not very strong, or very good walkers, the lady loaded with a basket containing two bottles of wine and a metal drinking-cup, and the gentleman carrying a heavy knapsack, filled with all sorts of odds and ends, strapped to his shoulders, should set off on a seven-mile walk, jump over a wall, run up a hillside, and yet feel in very good trim to enjoy a sunset view. This peculiar state of things I will proceed to explain.

I had been a professional man, but some years before had retired upon a very comfortable income. I had always been very fond of scientific pursuits, and now made these the occupation and pleasure of much of my leisure time. Our home was in a small town; and in a corner of my grounds I built a laboratory, where I carried on my work and my experiments. I had long been anxious to discover the means not only of producing, but of retaining and controlling, a natural force, really the same as centrifugal force, but which I called negative gravity. This name I adopted because it indicated better than any other the action of the force in question, as I produced it. Positive gravity attracts everything toward the centre of the earth. Negative gravity, therefore, would be that power which repels everything from the centre of the earth, just as the negative pole of a magnet repels the needle, while the positive pole attracts it. My object was, in fact, to store centrifugal force and to render it constant, controllable, and available for use. The advantages of such a discovery could scarcely be described. In a word, it would lighten the burdens of the world.

I will not touch upon the labors and disappointments of several years. It is enough to say that at last I discovered a method of producing, storing, and controlling negative gravity.

The mechanism of my invention was rather complicated, but the method of operating it was very simple. A strong metallic case, about eight inches long, and half as wide, contained the machinery for producing the force; and this was put into action by means of the pressure of a screw worked from the outside. As soon as this pressure was produced, negative gravity began to be evolved and stored, and the greater the pressure the greater the force. As the screw was moved outward, and the pressure diminished, the force decreased, and when the screw was withdrawn to its fullest extent, the action of negative gravity entirely ceased. Thus this force could be produced or dissipated at will to such degrees as might be desired, and its action, so long as the

requisite pressure was maintained, was constant.

When this little apparatus worked to my satis·
faction I called my wife into my laboratory and
explained to her my invention and its value. She
had known that I had been at work with an important object, but I had never told her what it
was. I had said that if I succeeded I would tell
her all, but if I failed she need not be troubled
with the matter at all. Being a very sensible
woman, this satisfied her perfectly. Now I explained everything to her — the construction of
the machine, and the wonderful uses to which
this invention could be applied. I told her that it
could diminish, or entirely dissipate, the weight
of objects of any kind. A heavily loaded wagon,
with two of these instruments fastened to its
sides, and each screwed to a proper force, would
be so lifted and supported that it would press
upon the ground as lightly as an empty cart, and
a small horse could draw it with ease. A bale of
cotton, with one of these machines attached,
could be handled and carried by a boy. A car,
with a number of these machines, could be made
to rise in the air like a balloon. Everything, in
fact, that was heavy could be made light; and as
a great part of labor, all over the world, is caused
by the attraction of gravitation, so this repellent
force, wherever applied, would make weight less
and work easier. I told her of many, many ways

in which the invention might be used, and would have told her of many more if she had not suddenly burst into tears.

" The world has gained something wonderful," she exclaimed, between her sobs, " but I have lost a husband! "

" What do you mean by that? " I asked, in surprise.

" I haven't minded it so far," she said, " because it gave you something to do, and it pleased you, and it never interfered with our home pleasures and our home life. But now that is all over. You will never be your own master again. It will succeed, I am sure, and you may make a great deal of money, but we don't need money. What we need is the happiness which we have always had until now. Now there will be companies, and patents, and lawsuits, and experiments, and people calling you a humbug, and other people saying they discovered it long ago, and all sorts of persons coming to see you, and you'll be obliged to go to all sorts of places, and you will be an altered man, and we shall never be happy again. Millions of money will not repay us for the happiness we have lost."

These words of my wife struck me with much force. Before I had called her my mind had begun to be filled and perplexed with ideas of what I ought to do now that the great invention was perfected. Until now the matter had not troubled

me at all. Sometimes I had gone backward and
sometimes forward, but, on the whole, I had always felt encouraged. I had taken great pleasure
in the work, but I had never allowed myself to be
too much absorbed by it. But now everything
was different. I began to feel that it was due to
myself and to my fellow-beings that I should
properly put this invention before the world.
And how should I set about it? What steps
should I take? I must make no mistakes. When
the matter should become known hundreds of
scientific people might set themselves to work;
how could I tell but that they might discover
other methods of producing the same effect? I
must guard myself against a great many things.
I must get patents in all parts of the world.
Already, as I have said, my mind began to be
troubled and perplexed with these things. A
turmoil of this sort did not suit my age or disposition. I could not but agree with my wife that
the joys of a quiet and contented life were now
about to be broken into.

"My dear," said I, "I believe, with you, that
the thing will do us more harm than good. If it
were not for depriving the world of the invention
I would throw the whole thing to the winds.
And yet," I added, regretfully, "I had expected
a great deal of personal gratification from the use
of this invention."

"Now listen," said my wife, eagerly; "don't

you think it would be best to do this: use the
thing as much as you please for your own amuse-
ment and satisfaction, but let the world wait? It
has waited a long time, and let it wait a little
longer.   When we are dead let Herbert have the
invention.   He will then be old enough to judge
for himself whether it will be better to take advantage of it for his own profit, or simply to give
it to the public for nothing.   It would be cheat-
ing him if we were to do the latter, but it would
also be doing him a great wrong if we were, at his
age, to load him with such a heavy responsibility.
Besides, if he took it up, you could not help going
into it, too."

I took my wife's advice.   I wrote a careful and
complete account of the invention, and, sealing it
up, I gave it to my lawyers to be handed to my
son after my death.   If he died first, I would
make other arrangements.   Then I determined to
get all the good and fun out of the thing that was
possible without telling any one anything about it.
Even Herbert, who was away from home, was not
to be told of the invention.

The first thing I did was to buy a strong
leathern knapsack, and inside of this I fastened
my little machine, with a screw so arranged that
it could be worked from the outside.   Strapping
this firmly to my shoulders, my wife gently turned
the screw at the back until the upward tendency
of the knapsack began to lift and sustain me.

When I felt myself so gently supported and up-
held that I seemed to weigh about thirty or forty
pounds, I would set out for a walk. The knapsack did not raise me from the ground, but it
gave me a very buoyant step. It was no labor at
all to walk; it was a delight, an ecstasy. With
the strength of a man and the weight of a child, I
gayly strode along. The first day I walked half
a dozen miles at a very brisk pace, and came back
without feeling in the least degree tired. These
walks now became one of the greatest joys of my
life. When nobody was looking, I would bound
over a fence, sometimes just touching it with one
hand, and sometimes not touching it at all. I delighted in rough places. I sprang over streams.
I jumped and I ran. I felt like Mercury himself.

I now set about making another machine, so
that my wife could accompany me in my walks;
but when it was finished she positively refused
to use it. " I can't wear a knapsack," she said,
" and there is no other good way of fastening it
to me. Besides, everybody about here knows I am
no walker, and it would only set them talking."

I occasionally made use of this second machine,
but I will give only one instance of its application.
Some repairs were needed to the foundation-walls
of my barn, and a two-horse wagon, loaded with
building-stone, had been brought into my yard
and left there. In the evening, when the men
had gone away, I took my two machines and

fastened them, with strong chains, one on each side of the loaded wagon. Then, gradually turning the screws, the wagon was so lifted that its weight became very greatly diminished. We had an old donkey which used to belong to Herbert, and which was now occasionally used with a small cart to bring packages from the station. I went into the barn and put the harness on the little fellow, and, bringing him out to the wagon, I attached him to it. In this position he looked very funny with a long pole sticking out in front of him and the great wagon behind him. When all was ready I touched him up; and, to my great delight, he moved off with the two-horse load of stone as easily as if he were drawing his own cart. I led him out into the public road, along which he proceeded without difficulty. He was an opinionated little beast, and sometimes stopped, not liking the peculiar manner in which he was harnessed; but a touch of the switch made him move on, and I soon turned him and brought the wagon back into the yard. This determined the success of my invention in one of its most important uses, and with a satisfied heart I put the donkey into the stable and went into the house.

Our trip to Europe was made a few months after this, and was mainly on our son Herbert's account. He, poor fellow, was in great trouble, and so, therefore, were we. He had become engaged, with our full consent, to a young lady in our town, the daughter of a gentleman whom we esteemed very highly. Herbert was young to be engaged to be married, but as we felt that he would never find a girl to make him so good a wife, we were entirely satisfied, especially as it was agreed on all hands that the marriage was not to take place for some time. It seemed to us that, in marrying Janet Gilbert, Herbert would secure for himself, in the very beginning of his career, the most important element of a happy life. But suddenly, without any reason that seemed to us justifiable, Mr. Gilbert, the only surviving parent of Janet, broke off the match; and he and his daughter soon after left the town for a trip to the West.

This blow nearly broke poor Herbert's heart. He gave up his professional studies and came home to us, and for a time we thought he would be seriously ill. Then we took him to Europe, and after a Continental tour of a month or two we left him, at his own request, in Göttingen, where he thought it would do him good to go to work again. Then we went down to the little town in Italy where my story first finds us. My wife had suffered much in mind and body on her son's account, and for this reason I was anxious that she should take outdoor exercise, and enjoy as much as possible the bracing air of the country. I had brought with me both my little machines. One was still in my knapsack, and the other I had fastened to the inside of an enormous family trunk. As one is obliged to pay for nearly every pound of his baggage on the Continent, this saved me a great deal of money. Everything heavy was packed into this great trunk — books, papers, the bronze, iron, and marble relics we had picked up, and all the articles that usually weigh down a tourist's baggage. I screwed up the negative-gravity apparatus until the trunk could be handled with great ease by an ordinary porter. I could have made it weigh nothing at all, but this, of course, I did not wish to do. The lightness of my baggage, however, had occasioned some comment, and I had overheard remarks which were not altogether complimentary about people travelling around with empty trunks; but this only amused me.

Desirous that my wife should have the advantage of negative gravity while taking our walks, I had removed the machine from the trunk and fastened it inside of the basket, which she could carry under her arm. This assisted her wonderfully. When one arm was tired she put the basket under the other, and thus, with one hand on my arm, she could easily keep up with the free and buoyant steps my knapsack enabled me to take. She did not object to long tramps here, because nobody knew that she was not a walker, and she always carried some wine or other refreshment in the basket, not only because it was pleasant to have it with us, but because it seemed ridiculous to go about carrying an empty basket.

There were English-speaking people stopping at the hotel where we were, but they seemed more fond of driving than walking, and none of them offered to accompany us on our rambles, for which we were very glad. There was one man there, however, who was a great walker. He was an Englishman, a member of an Alpine Club, and generally went about dressed in a knickerbocker suit, with gray woollen stockings covering an enormous pair of calves. One evening this gentleman was talking to me and some others about the ascent of the Matterhorn, and I took occasion to deliver in pretty strong language my opinion upon such exploits. I declared them to be useless, foolhardy, and, if the climber had any one who loved him, wicked.

" Even if the weather should permit a view," I said, " what is that compared to the terrible risk to life? Under certain circumstances," I added (thinking of a kind of waistcoat I had some idea of making, which, set about with little negative-gravity machines, all connected with a conveniently handled screw, would enable the wearer at times to dispense with his weight altogether), " such ascents might be divested of danger, and be quite admissible; but ordinarily they should be frowned upon by the intelligent public."

The Alpine Club man looked at me, especially

regarding my somewhat slight figure and thinnish legs.

"It's all very well for you to talk that way," he said, "because it is easy to see that you are not up to that sort of thing."

"In conversations of this kind," I replied, "I never make personal allusions; but since you have chosen to do so, I feel inclined to invite you to walk with me to-morrow to the top of the mountain to the north of this town."

"I'll do it," he said, "at any time you choose to name." And as I left the room soon afterward I heard him laugh.

The next afternoon, about two o'clock, the Alpine Club man and myself set out for the mountain.

"What have you got in your knapsack?" he said.

"A hammer to use if I come across geological specimens, a field-glass, a flask of wine, and some other things."

"I wouldn't carry any weight, if I were you," he said.

"Oh, I don't mind it," I answered, and off we started.

The mountain to which we were bound was about two miles from the town. Its nearest side was steep, and in places almost precipitous, but it sloped away more gradually toward the north, and up that side a road led by devious windings to a village near the summit. It was not a very high mountain, but it would do for an afternoon's climb.

" I suppose you want to go up by the road," said my companion.

" Oh no," I answered, " we won't go so far around as that. There is a path up this side, along which I have seen men driving their goats. I prefer to take that."

" All right, if you say so," he answered, with a smile; " but you'll find it pretty tough."

After a time he remarked:

" I wouldn't walk so fast, if I were you."

" Oh, I like to step along briskly," I said. And briskly on we went.

My wife had screwed up the machine in the knapsack more than usual, and walking seemed scarcely any effort at all. I carried a long alpenstock, and when we reached the mountain and began the ascent, I found that with the help of this and my knapsack I could go uphill at a wonderful rate. My companion had taken the lead, so as to show me how to climb. Making a *détour* over some rocks, I quickly passed him and went ahead. After that it was impossible for him to keep up with me. I ran up steep places, I cut off the windings of the path by lightly clambering over rocks, and even when I followed the beaten track my step was as rapid as if I had been walking on level ground.

"Look here!" shouted the Alpine Club man from below, "you'll kill yourself if you go at that rate! That's no way to climb mountains."

"It's my way!" I cried. And on I skipped.

Twenty minutes after I arrived at the summit my companion joined me, puffing, and wiping his red face with his handkerchief.

"Confound it!" he cried, "I never came up a mountain so fast in my life."

"You need not have hurried," I said, coolly.

"I was afraid something would happen to you," he growled, "and I wanted to stop you. I never saw a person climb in such an utterly absurd way."

"I don't see why you should call it absurd," I said, smiling with an air of superiority. "I arrived here in a perfectly comfortable condition, neither heated nor wearied."

He made no answer, but walked off to a little distance, fanning himself with his hat and growling words which I did not catch. After a time I proposed to descend.

"You must be careful as you go down," he said. "It is much more dangerous to go down steep places than to climb up."

"I am always prudent," I answered, and started in advance. I found the descent of the mountain much more pleasant than the ascent. It was positively exhilarating. I jumped from rocks and bluffs eight and ten feet in height, and touched the ground as gently as if I had stepped down but two feet. I ran down steep paths, and, with the aid of my alpenstock, stopped myself in an instant. I was careful to avoid dangerous places, but the runs and jumps I made were such as no man had ever made before upon that mountain-side. Once only I heard my companion's voice.

" You'll break your —— neck! " he yelled.

" Never fear! " I called back, and soon left him far above.

When I reached the bottom I would have waited for him, but my activity had warmed me up, and as a cool evening breeze was beginning to blow I thought it better not to stop and take cold. Half an hour after my arrival at the hotel I came down to the court, cool, fresh, and dressed for dinner, and just in time to meet the Alpine man as he entered, hot, dusty, and growling.

" Excuse me for not waiting for you," I said; but without stopping to hear my reason, he muttered something about waiting in a place where no one would care to stay, and passed into the house.

There was no doubt that what I had done gratified my pique and tickled my vanity.

" I think now," I said, when I related the matter to my wife, " that he will scarcely say that I am not up to that sort of thing."

" I am not sure," she answered, " that it was

exactly fair. He did not know how you were assisted."

"It was fair enough," I said. "He is enabled to climb well by the inherited vigor of his constitution and by his training. He did not tell me what methods of exercise he used to get those great muscles upon his legs. I am enabled to climb by the exercise of my intellect. My method is my business and his method is his business. It is all perfectly fair."

Still she persisted:

"He *thought* that you climbed with your legs, and not with your head."

And now, after this long digression, necessary to explain how a middle-aged couple of slight pedestrian ability, and loaded with a heavy knapsack and basket, should have started out on a rough walk and climb, fourteen miles in all, we will return to ourselves, standing on the little bluff and gazing out upon the sunset view. When the sky began to fade a little we turned from it and prepared to go back to the town.

"Where is the basket?" I said.

"I left it right here," answered my wife. "I unscrewed the machine and it lay perfectly flat."

"Did you afterward take out the bottles?" I asked, seeing them lying on the grass.

"Yes, I believe I did. I had to take out yours in order to get at mine."

"Then," said I, after looking all about the

grassy patch on which we stood, " I am afraid you did not entirely unscrew the instrument, and that when the weight of the bottles was removed the basket gently rose into the air."

" It may be so," she said, lugubriously. " The basket was behind me as I drank my wine."

" I believe that is just what has happened," I said. " Look up there! I vow that is our basket! "

I pulled out my field-glass and directed it at a little speck high above our heads. It was the basket floating high in the air. I gave the glass to my wife to look, but she did not want to use it.

" What shall I do? " she cried. " I can't walk home without that basket. It's perfectly dreadful! " And she looked as if she was going to cry.

" Do not distress yourself," I said, although I was a good deal disturbed myself. " We shall get home very well. You shall put your hand on my shoulder, while I put my arm around you. Then you can screw up my machine a good deal higher, and it will support us both. In this way I am sure that we shall get on very well."

We carried out this plan, and managed to walk on with moderate comfort. To be sure, with the knapsack pulling me upward, and the weight of my wife pulling me down, the straps hurt me somewhat, which they had not done before. We did not spring lightly over the wall into the road,

but, still clinging to each other, we clambered
awkwardly over it.   The road for the most part
declined gently toward the town, and with moderate ease we made our way along it.   But we
walked much more slowly than we had done before, and it was quite dark when we reached our
hotel.   If it had not been for the light inside the
court it would have been difficult for us to find it.
A travelling-carriage was standing before the entrance, and against the light.   It was necessary
to pass around it, and my wife went first.   I attempted to follow her, but, strange to say, there
was nothing under my feet.   I stepped vigorously, but only wagged my legs in the air.   To
my horror I found that I was rising in the air!   I
soon saw, by the light below me, that I was some
fifteen feet from the ground.   The carriage drove
away, and in the darkness I was not noticed.   Of
course I knew what had happened.   The instrument in my knapsack had been screwed up to such
an intensity, in order to support both myself and
my wife, that when her weight was removed the
force of the negative gravity was sufficient to raise
me from the ground.   But I was glad to find that
when I had risen to the height I have mentioned
I did not go up any higher, but hung in the air,
about on a level with the second tier of windows
of the hotel.

I now began to try to reach the screw in my
knapsack in order to reduce the force of the neg-

ative gravity; but, do what I would, I could not get my hand to it. The machine in the knapsack had been placed so as to support me in a well-balanced and comfortable way; and in doing this it had been impossible to set the screw so that I could reach it. But in a temporary arrangement of the kind this had not been considered necessary, as my wife always turned the screw for me until sufficient lifting power had been attained. I had intended, as I have said before, to construct a negative-gravity waistcoat, in which the screw should be in front, and entirely under the wearer's control; but this was a thing of the future.

When I found that I could not turn the screw I began to be much alarmed. Here I was, dangling in the air, without any means of reaching the ground. I could not expect my wife to return to look for me, as she would naturally suppose I had stopped to speak to some one. I thought of loosening myself from the knapsack, but this would not do, for I should fall heavily, and either kill myself or break some of my bones. I did not dare to call for assistance, for if any of the simple-minded inhabitants of the town had discovered me floating in the air they would have taken me for a demon, and would probably have shot at me. A moderate breeze was blowing, and it wafted me gently down the street. If it had blown me against a tree I would have seized it, and have endeavored, so to speak, to climb down

it; but there were no trees. There was a dim
street-lamp here and there, but reflectors above
them threw their light upon the pavement, and
none up to me. On many accounts I was glad
that the night was so dark, for, much as I desired
to get down, I wanted no one to see me in my
strange position, which, to any one but myself
and wife, would be utterly unaccountable. If I
could rise as high as the roofs I might get on
one of them, and, tearing off an armful of tiles,
so load myself that I would be heavy enough to
descend. But I did not rise to the eaves of any
of the houses. If there had been a telegraph-
pole, or anything of the kind that I could have
clung to, I would have taken off the knapsack,
and would have endeavored to scramble down as
well as I could. But there was nothing I could
cling to. Even the water-spouts, if I could have
reached the face of the houses, were embedded in
the walls. At an open window, near which I was
slowly blown, I saw two little boys going to bed
by the light of a dim candle. I was dreadfully
afraid that they would see me and raise an alarm.
I actually came so near to the window that I
threw out one foot and pushed against the wall
with such force that I went nearly across the
street. I thought I caught sight of a frightened
look on the face of one of the boys; but of this I
am not sure, and I heard no cries. I still floated,
dangling, down the street. What was to be done?

Should I call out? In that case, if I were not shot or stoned, my strange predicament, and the secret of my invention, would be exposed to the world. If I did not do this, I must either let myself drop and be killed or mangled, or hang there and die. When, during the course of the night, the air became more rarefied, I might rise higher and higher, perhaps to an altitude of one or two hundred feet. It would then be impossible for the people to reach me and get me down, even if they were convinced that I was not a demon. I should then expire, and when the birds of the air had eaten all of me that they could devour, I should forever hang above the unlucky town, a dangling skeleton with a knapsack on its back.

Such thoughts were not reassuring, and I determined that if I could find no means of getting down without assistance, I would call out and run all risks; but so long as I could endure the tension of the straps I would hold out, and hope for a tree or a pole. Perhaps it might rain, and my wet clothes would then become so heavy that I would descend as low as the top of a lamp-post.

As this thought was passing through my mind I saw a spark of light upon the street approaching me. I rightly imagined that it came from a tobacco-pipe, and presently I heard a voice. It was that of the Alpine Club man. Of all people in the world I did not want him to discover me, and I hung as motionless as possible. The man was speaking to another person who was walking with him.

"He is crazy beyond a doubt," said the Alpine man. "Nobody but a maniac could have gone up and down that mountain as he did! He hasn't any muscles, and one need only look at him to know that he couldn't do any climbing in a natural way. It is only the excitement of insanity that gives him strength."

The two now stopped almost under me, and the speaker continued:

"Such things are very common with maniacs. At times they acquire an unnatural strength which is perfectly wonderful. I have seen a little fellow struggle and fight so that four strong men could not hold him."

Then the other person spoke.

"I am afraid what you say is too true," he remarked. "Indeed, I have known it for some time."

At these words my breath almost stopped. It was the voice of Mr. Gilbert, my townsman, and the father of Janet. It must have been he who had arrived in the travelling-carriage. He was acquainted with the Alpine Club man, and they were talking of me. Proper or improper, I listened with all my ears.

"It is a very sad case," Mr. Gilbert continued. "My daughter was engaged to marry his son, but I broke off the match. I could not have her marry the son of a lunatic, and there could be no doubt of his condition. He has been seen—a man of his age, and the head of a family—to load himself up with a heavy knapsack, which there was no earthly necessity for him to carry, and go skipping along the road for miles, vaulting over fences and jumping over rocks and ditches like a young calf or a colt. I myself saw a most heartrending instance of how a kindly man's nature can be changed by the derangement of his intellect. I was at some distance from his house, but I plainly saw him harness a little donkey which he owns to a large two-horse wagon loaded with stone, and beat and lash the poor little beast until it drew the heavy load some distance along the public road. I would have remonstrated with him on this horrible cruelty, but he had the wagon back in his yard before I could reach him."

" Oh, there can be no doubt of his insanity," said the Alpine Club man, " and he oughtn't to be allowed to travel about in this way. Some day he will pitch his wife over a precipice just for the fun of seeing her shoot through the air."

" I am sorry he is here," said Mr. Gilbert, " for it would be very painful to meet him. My daughter and I will retire very soon, and go away as early to-morrow morning as possible, so as to avoid seeing him."

And then they walked back to the hotel.

For a few moments I hung, utterly forgetful of my condition, and absorbed in the consideration of these revelations. One idea now filled my mind. Everything must be explained to Mr. Gilbert, even if it should be necessary to have him called to me, and for me to speak to him from the upper air.

Just then I saw something white approaching me along the road. My eyes had become accustomed to the darkness, and I perceived that it was an upturned face. I recognized the hurried gait, the form; it was my wife. As she came near me, I called her name, and in the same breath entreated her not to scream. It must have been an effort for her to restrain herself, but she did it.

"You must help me to get down," I said, "without anybody seeing us."

"What shall I do?" she whispered.

"Try to catch hold of this string."

Taking a piece of twine from my pocket, I lowered one end to her. But it was too short; she could not reach it. I then tied my handkerchief to it, but still it was not long enough.

"I can get more string, or handkerchiefs," she whispered, hurriedly.

"No," I said; "you could not get them up to me. But, leaning against the hotel wall, on this side, in the corner, just inside of the garden gate, are some fishing-poles. I have seen them there every day. You can easily find them in the dark. Go, please, and bring me one of those."

The hotel was not far away, and in a few minutes my wife returned with a fishing-pole. She stood on tiptoe, and reached it high in air; but all she could do was to strike my feet and legs with it. My most frantic exertions did not enable me to get my hands low enough to touch it.

"Wait a minute," she said; and the rod was withdrawn.

I knew what she was doing. There was a hook and line attached to the pole, and with womanly dexterity she was fastening the hook to the extreme end of the rod. Soon she reached up, and gently struck at my legs. After a few attempts the hook caught in my trousers, a little below my right knee. Then there was a slight pull, a long scratch down my leg, and the hook was stopped by the top of my boot. Then came a steady downward pull, and I felt myself descending. Gently and firmly the rod was drawn down; carefully the lower end was kept free from the ground; and in a few moments my ankle was seized with a vigorous grasp. Then some one seemed to climb up me, my feet touched the ground, an arm was thrown around my neck, the hand of another arm was busy at the back of my knapsack, and I soon stood firmly in the road, entirely divested of negative gravity.

"Oh that I should have forgotten," sobbed my wife, "and that I should have dropped your arms and let you go up into the air! At first I thought that you had stopped below, and it was only a little while ago that the truth flashed upon me. Then I rushed out and began looking up for you. I knew that you had wax matches in your pocket, and hoped that you would keep on striking them, so that you would be seen."

" But I did not wish to be seen," I said, as we hurried to the hotel; " and I can never be sufficiently thankful that it was you who found me and brought me down. Do you know that it is Mr. Gilbert and his daughter who have just arrived? I must see him instantly. I will explain it all to you when I come upstairs."

I took off my knapsack and gave it to my wife, who carried it to our room, while I went to look for Mr. Gilbert. Fortunately I found him just as he was about to go up to his chamber. He took my offered hand, but looked at me sadly and gravely.

" Mr. Gilbert," I said, " I must speak to you in private. Let us step into this room. There is no one here."

" My friend," said Mr. Gilbert, " it will be much better to avoid discussing this subject. It is very painful to both of us, and no good can come from talking of it."

" You cannot now comprehend what it is I want to say to you," I replied. " Come in here, and in a few minutes you will be very glad that you listened to me."

My manner was so earnest and impressive that

Mr. Gilbert was constrained to follow me, and we went into a small room called the smoking-room, but in which people seldom smoked, and closed the door. I immediately began my statement. I told my old friend that I had discovered, by means that I need not explain at present, that he had considered me crazy, and that now the most important object of my life was to set myself right in his eyes. I thereupon gave him the whole history of my invention, and explained the reason of the actions that had appeared to him those of a lunatic. I said nothing about the little incident of that evening. That was a mere accident, and I did not care now to speak of it.

Mr. Gilbert listened to me very attentively.

"Your wife is here?" he asked, when I had finished.

"Yes," I said; "and she will corroborate my story in every item, and no one could ever suspect her of being crazy. I will go and bring her to you."

In a few minutes my wife was in the room, had shaken hands with Mr. Gilbert, and had been told of my suspected madness. She turned pale, but smiled.

"He did act like a crazy man," she said, "but I never supposed that anybody would think him one." And tears came into her eyes.

"And now, my dear," said I, "perhaps you will tell Mr. Gilbert how I did all this."

And then she told him the story that I had told.

Mr. Gilbert looked from the one to the other of us with a troubled air.

"Of course I do not doubt either of you, or rather I do not doubt that you believe what you say. All would be right if I could bring myself to credit that such a force as that you speak of can possibly exist."

"That is a matter," said I, "which I can easily prove to you by actual demonstration. If you can wait a short time, until my wife and I have had something to eat—for I am nearly famished, and I am sure she must be—I will set your mind at rest upon that point."

"I will wait here," said Mr. Gilbert, "and smoke a cigar. Don't hurry yourselves. I shall be glad to have some time to think about what you have told me."

When we had finished the dinner, which had been set aside for us, I went upstairs and got my knapsack, and we both joined Mr. Gilbert in the smoking-room. I showed him the little machine, and explained, very briefly, the principle of its construction. I did not give any practical demonstration of its action, because there were people walking about the corridor who might at any moment come into the room; but, looking out of the window, I saw that the night was much clearer. The wind had dissipated the clouds, and the stars were shining brightly.

" If you will come up the street with me," said
I to Mr. Gilbert, " I will show you how this thing
works."

" That is just what I want to see," he answered.

" I will go with you," said my wife, throwing
a shawl over her head. And we started up the
street.

When we were outside the little town I found
the starlight was quite sufficient for my purppse.
The white roadway, the low walls, and objects
about us, could easily be distinguished.

" Now," said I to Mr. Gilbert, " I want to put
this knapsack on you, and let you see how it
feels, and how it will help you to walk." To
this he assented with some eagerness, and I
strapped it firmly on him. " I will now turn
this screw," said I, " until you shall become
lighter and lighter."

" Be very careful not to turn it too much," said
my wife, earnestly.

" Oh, you may depend on me for that," said
I, turning the screw very gradually.

Mr. Gilbert was a stout man, and I was obliged
to give the screw a good many turns.

" There seems to be considerable hoist in it,"
he said, directly. And then I put my arms around
him, and found that I could raise him from the
ground.

" Are you lifting me? " he exclaimed, in surprise.

"Yes; I did it with ease," I answered.

"Upon — my — word!" ejaculated Mr. Gilbert.

I then gave the screw a half-turn more, and told him to walk and run. He started off, at first slowly, then he made long strides, then he began to run, and then to skip and jump. It had been many years since Mr. Gilbert had skipped and jumped. No one was in sight, and he was free to gambol as much as he pleased. "Could you give it another turn?" said he, bounding up to me. "I want to try that wall." I put on a little more negative gravity, and he vaulted over a five-foot wall with great ease. In an instant he had leaped back into the road, and in two bounds was at my side. "I came down as light as a cat," he said. "There was never anything like it." And away he went up the road, taking steps at least eight feet long, leaving my wife and me laughing heartily at the preternatural agility of our stout friend. In a few minutes he was with us again. "Take it off," he said. "If I wear it any longer I shall want one myself, and then I shall be taken for a crazy man, and perhaps clapped into an asylum."

"Now," said I, as I turned back the screw before unstrapping the knapsack, "do you understand how I took long walks, and leaped and jumped; how I ran uphill and downhill, and how the little donkey drew the loaded wagon?"

" I understand it all," cried he. " I take back all I ever said or thought about you, my friend."

"And Herbert may marry Janet?" cried my wife.

" *May* marry her! " cried Mr. Gilbert. " Indeed, he *shall* marry her, if I have anything to say about it! My poor girl has been drooping ever since I told her it could not be."

My wife rushed at him, but whether she embraced him or only shook his hands I cannot say; for I had the knapsack in one hand and was rubbing my eyes with the other.

" But, my dear fellow," said Mr. Gilbert, directly, " if you still consider it to your interest to keep your invention a secret, I wish you had never made it. No one having a machine like that can help using it, and it is often quite as bad to be considered a maniac as to be one."

" My friend," I cried, with some excitement, " I have made up my mind on this subject. The little machine in this knapsack, which is the only one I now possess, has been a great pleasure to me. But I now know it has also been of the greatest injury indirectly to me and mine, not to mention some direct inconvenience and danger, which I will speak of another time. The secret lies with us three, and we will keep it. But the invention itself is too full of temptation and danger for any of us."

As I said this I held the knapsack with one hand while I quickly turned the screw with the other. In a few moments it was high above my head, while I with difficulty held it down by the straps. "Look!" I cried. And then I released my hold, and the knapsack shot into the air and disappeared into the upper gloom.

I was about to make a remark, but had no chance, for my wife threw herself upon my bosom, sobbing with joy.

"Oh, I am so glad—so glad!" she said. "And you will never make another?"

"Never another!" I answered.

"And now let us hurry in and see Janet," said my wife.

"You don't know how heavy and clumsy I feel," said Mr. Gilbert, striving to keep up with us as we walked back. "If I had worn that thing much longer, I should never have been willing to take it off!"

Janet had retired, but my wife went up to her room.

"I think she has felt it as much as our boy," she said, when she rejoined me. "But I tell you, my dear, I left a very happy girl in that little bedchamber over the garden."

And there were three very happy elderly people talking together until quite late that evening. "I shall write to Herbert to-night," I said, when we separated, "and tell him to meet us all in Geneva. It will do the young man no harm if we interrupt his studies just now."

"You must let me add a postscript to the letter," said Mr. Gilbert, "and I am sure it will require no knapsack with a screw in the back to bring him quickly to us."

And it did not.

There is a wonderful pleasure in tripping over the earth like a winged Mercury, and in feeling one's self relieved of much of that attraction of gravitation which drags us down to earth and gradually makes the movement of our bodies but weariness and labor. But this pleasure is not to be compared, I think, to that given by the buoyancy and lightness of two young and loving hearts, reunited after a separation which they had supposed would last forever.

What became of the basket and the knapsack, or whether they ever met in upper air, I do not know. If they but float away and stay away from ken of mortal man, I shall be satisfied.

And whether or not the world will ever know more of the power of negative gravity depends entirely upon the disposition of my son Herbert, when — after a good many years, I hope — he shall open the packet my lawyers have in keeping.

[NOTE.— It would be quite useless for any one to interview my wife on this subject, for she has entirely forgotten how my machine was made. And as for Mr. Gilbert, he never knew.]

ASAPH

ASAPH

BOUT a hundred feet back from the main street of a village in New Jersey there stood a very good white house. Half-way between it and the sidewalk was a large chestnut-tree, which had been the pride of Mr. Himes, who built the house, and was now the pride of Mrs. Himes, his widow, who lived there.

Under the tree was a bench, and on the bench were two elderly men, both smoking pipes, and each one of them leaning forward with his elbows on his knees. One of these, Thomas Rooper by name, was a small man with gray side-whiskers, a rather thin face, and very good clothes. His pipe was a meerschaum, handsomely colored, with a long amber tip. He had bought that pipe while on a visit to Philadelphia during the great Centennial Exposition; and if any one noticed it and happened to remark what a fine pipe it was, that person would be likely to receive a detailed account of the circumstances of its purchase, with an appendix relating to the Main Building, the Art Building, the Agricultural Building, and many other salient points of the great Exposition which commemorated the centennial of our national independence.

The other man, Asaph Scantle, was of a different type. He was a little older than his companion, but if his hair were gray, it did not show very much, as his rather long locks were of a sandy hue and his full face was clean shaven, at least on Wednesdays and Sundays. He was tall, round-shouldered, and his clothes were not good, possessing very evident claims to a position on the retired list. His pipe consisted of a common clay bowl with a long reed stem.

For some minutes the two men continued to puff together as if they were playing a duet upon tobacco-pipes, and then Asaph, removing his reed from his lips, remarked, " What you ought to do, Thomas, is to marry money."

" There's sense in that," replied the other; " but you wasn't the first to think of it."

Asaph, who knew very well that Mr. Rooper never allowed any one to suppose that he received suggestions from without, took no notice of the last remark, but went on : " Lookin' at the matter in a friendly way, it seems to me it stands to reason that when the shingles on a man's house is so rotten that the rain comes through into every room

on the top floor, and when the plaster on the
ceilin' is tumblin' down more or less all the time,
and the window-sashes is all loose, and things
generally in a condition that he can't let that
house without spendin' at least a year's rent on it
to git it into decent order, and when a man's got
to the time of life—"

" There's nothin' the matter with the time of
life," said Thomas; " that's all right."

" What I was goin' to say was," continued
Asaph, " that when a man gits to the time of life
when he knows what it is to be comfortable in his
mind as well as his body — and that time comes to
sensible people as soon as they git fairly growed
up — he don't want to give up his good room in
the tavern and all the privileges of the house, and
go to live on his own property and have the
plaster come down on his own head and the rain
come down on the coverlet of his own bed."

" No, he don't," said Thomas; " and what is
more, he isn't goin' to do it.   But what I git
from the rent of that house is what I have to live
on; there's no gittin' around that pint."

" Well, then," said Asaph, " if you don't marry
money, what are you goin' to do?   You can't go
back to your old business."

" I never had but one business," said Thomas.
" I lived with my folks until I was a good deal
more than growed up; and when the war broke
out I went as sutler to the rigiment from this

place; and all the money I made I put into my
property in the village here. That's what I've
lived on ever since. There's no more war, so
there's no more sutlers, except away out West
where I wouldn't go; and there are no more
folks, for they are all dead; and if what Mrs.
McJimsey says is true, there'll be no more ten-
ants in my house after the 1st of next November.
For when the McJimseys go on account of want of
general repairs, it is not to be expected that anybody else will come there. There's nobody in this
place that can stand as much as the McJimseys can."

"Consequently," said Asaph, deliberately filling his pipe, "it stands to reason that there ain't
nothin' for you to do but marry money."

Thomas Rooper took his pipe from his mouth
and sat up straight. Gazing steadfastly at his
companion, he remarked, "If you think that is
such a good thing to do, why don't you do it
yourself? There can't be anybody much harder
up than you are."

"The law's agin' my doin' it," said Asaph.
"A man can't marry his sister."

"Are you thinkin' of Marietta Himes?" asked
Mr. Rooper.

"That's the one I'm thinkin' of," said Asaph.
"If you can think of anybody better, I'd like you
to mention her."

Mr. Rooper did not immediately speak. He
presently asked, "What do you call money?"

" Well," said Asaph, with a little hesitation,
" considerin' the circumstances, I should say that
in a case like this about fifteen hundred a year, a
first-rate house with not a loose shingle on it nor
a crack anywhere, a good garden and an orchard,
two cows, a piece of meadow-land on the other
side of the creek, and all the clothes a woman
need have, is money."

Thomas shrugged his shoulders. " Clothes! "
he said. " If she marries she'll go out of black,
and then she'll have to have new ones, and lot's
of 'em. That would make a big hole in her
money, Asaph."

The other smiled. " I always knowed you was
a far-seein' feller, Thomas; but it stands to reason
that Marietta's got a lot of clothes that was on
hand before she went into mournin', and she's
not the kind of woman to waste 'em. She'll be
twistin' 'em about and makin' 'em over to suit
the fashions, and it won't be like her to be buyin'
new colored goods when she's got plenty of 'em
already."

There was now another pause in the conversation, and then Mr. Rooper remarked, " Mrs.
Himes must be gettin' on pretty well in years."

" She's not a young woman," said Asaph; " but
if she was much younger she wouldn't have you,
and if she was much older you wouldn't have
her. So it strikes me she's just about the right
pint."

" How old was John Himes when he died? "
asked Thomas.

" I don't exactly know that; but he was a lot
older than Marietta."

Thomas shook his head. " It strikes me,"
said he, " that John Himes had a hearty constitution and hadn't ought to died as soon as he did.
He fell away a good deal in the last years of his
life."

" And considerin' that he died of consumption,
he had a right to fall away," said Asaph. " If
what you are drivin' at, Thomas, is that Marietta
isn't a good housekeeper and hasn't the right sort
of notions of feedin', look at me. I've lived with
Marietta just about a year, and in that time I have
gained forty-two pounds. Now, of course, I ain't
unreasonable, and don't mean to say that you
would gain forty-two pounds in a year, 'cause you
ain't got the frame and bone to put it on; but it
wouldn't surprise me a bit if you was to gain
twenty, or even twenty-five, pounds in eighteen
months, anyway; and more than that you ought
not to ask, Thomas, considerin' your height and
general build."

" Isn't Marietta Himes a good deal of a free-
thinker? " asked Thomas.

" A what? " cried Asaph. " You mean an in-
fidel? "

" No," said Thomas, " I don't charge nobody
with nothin' more than there's reason for; but

they do say that she goes sometimes to one church and sometimes to another, and that if there was a Catholic church in this village she would go to that. And who's goin' to say where a woman will turn up when she don't know her own mind better than that?"

Asaph colored a little. "The place where Marietta will turn up," said he, warmly, "is on a front seat in the kingdom of heaven; and if the people that talk about her will mend their ways, they'll see that I am right. You need not trouble yourself about that, Thomas. Marietta Himes is pious to the heel."

Mr. Rooper now shifted himself a little on the bench and crossed one leg over the other. "Now look here, Asaph," he said, with a little more animation than he had yet shown, "supposin' all you say is true, have you got any reason to think that Mrs. Himes ain't satisfied with things as they are?"

"Yes, I have," said Asaph. "And I don't mind tellin' you that the thing she's least satisfied with is me. She wants a man in the house; that is nateral. She wouldn't be Marietta Himes if she didn't. When I come to live with her I thought the whole business was settled; but it isn't. I don't suit her. I don't say she's lookin' for another man, but if another man was to come along, and if he was the right kind of a man, it's my opinion she's ready for him. I wouldn't say

this to everybody, but I say it to you, Thomas
Rooper, 'cause I know what kind of a man you are."

Mr. Rooper did not return the compliment.
" I don't wonder your sister ain't satisfied with
you," he said, " for you go ahead of all the lazy
men I ever saw yet. They was sayin' down at
the tavern yesterday — only yesterday — that you
could do less work in more time than anybody
they ever saw before."

"There's two ways of workin'," said Asaph.
" Some people work with their hands and some
with their heads."

Thomas grimly smiled. " It strikes me," said
he, " that the most head-work you do is with your
jaws."

Asaph was not the man to take offence readily,
especially when he considered it against his interest to do so, and he showed no resentment at this
remark. " 'Tain't so much my not makin' myself more generally useful," he said, " that Marietta objects to; though, of course, it could not be
expected that a man that hasn't got any interest
in property would keep workin' at it like a man
that has got an interest in it, such as Marietta's
husband would have; but it's my general appearance that she don't like. She's told me more than
once she didn't so much mind my bein' lazy as
lookin' lazy."

" I don't wonder she thinks that way," said
Thomas. " But look here, Asaph, do you sup-

pose that if Marietta Himes was to marry a man,
he would really come into her property?"

"There ain't nobody that knows my sister better than I know her, and I can say, without any
fear of bein' contradicted, that when she gives
herself to a man the good-will and fixtures will be
included."

Thomas Rooper now leaned forward with his
elbows on his knees without smoking, and Asaph
Scantle leaned forward with his elbows on his
knees without smoking. And thus they remained,
saying nothing to each other, for the space of some
ten minutes.

Asaph was a man who truly used his head a
great deal more than he used his hands. He
had always been a shiftless fellow, but he was no
fool, and this his sister found out soon after she
asked him to come and make his home with her.
She had not done this because she wanted a man
in the house, for she had lived two or three years
without that convenience and had not felt the
need of it. But she heard that Asaph was in
very uncomfortable circumstances, and she had
sent for him solely for his own good. The arrangement proved to be a very good one for her
brother, but not a good one for her. She had
always known that Asaph's head was his main
dependence, but she was just beginning to discover that he liked to use his head so that other
people's hands should work for him.

"There ain't nobody comin' to see your sister, is there?" asked Thomas, suddenly.

"Not a livin' soul," said Asaph, "except women, married folk, and children. But it has always surprised me that nobody did come; but just at this minute the field's clear and the gate's open."

"Well," said Mr. Rooper, "I'll think about it."

"That's right," said Asaph, rubbing his knees with his hands. "That's right. But now tell me, Thomas Rooper, supposin' you get Marietta, what are you goin' to do for me?"

"For you?" exclaimed the other. "What have you got to do with it?"

"A good deal," said Asaph. "If you get Marietta with her fifteen hundred a year—and it wouldn't surprise me if it was eighteen hundred —and her house and her garden and her cattle and her field and her furniture, with not a leg ·loose nor a scratch, you will get her because I proposed her to you, and because I backed you up afterward. And now, then, I want to know what you are goin' to do for me?"

"What do you want?" asked Thomas.

"The first thing I want," said Asaph, "is a suit of clothes. These clothes is disgraceful."

"You are right there," said Mr. Rooper. "I wonder your sister lets you come around in front of the house. But what do you mean by clothes — winter clothes or summer clothes?"

"Winter," said Asaph, without hesitation. "I don't count summer clothes. And when I say a suit of clothes, I mean shoes and hat and under-clothes."

Mr. Rooper gave a sniff. "I wonder you don't say overcoat," he remarked.

"I do say overcoat," replied Asaph. "A suit of winter clothes is a suit of clothes that you can go out into the weather in without missin' nothin'."

Mr. Rooper smiled sarcastically. "Is there anything else you want?" he asked.

"Yes," said Asaph, decidedly; "there is. I want a umbrella."

"Cotton or silk?"

Asaph hesitated. He had never had a silk umbrella in his hand in his life. He was afraid to strike too high, and he answered, "I want a good stout gingham."

Mr. Rooper nodded his head. "Very good," he said. "And is that all?"

"No," said Asaph, "it ain't all. There is one more thing I want, and that is a dictionary."

The other man rose to his feet. "Upon my word," he exclaimed, "I never before saw a man that would sell his sister for a dictionary! And what you want with a dictionary is past my con-ceivin'."

"Well, it ain't past mine," said Asaph. "For more than ten years I have wanted a dictionary. If I had a dictionary I could make use of my head in a way that I can't now. There is books in this house, but amongst 'em there is no dictionary. If there had been one I'd been a different man by this time from what I am now, and like as not Marietta wouldn't have wanted any other man in the house but me."

Mr. Rooper stood looking upon the ground; and Asaph, who had also arisen, waited for him to speak. "You are a graspin' man, Asaph," said Thomas. "But there is another thing I'd like to know: if I give you them clothes, you don't want them before she's married?"

"Yes, I do," said Asaph. "If I come to the weddin', I can't wear these things. I have got to have them first."

Mr. Rooper gave his head a little twist. "There's many a slip 'twixt the cup and the lip," said he.

"Yes," said Asaph; "and there's different cups and different lips. But what's more, if I was to be best man — which would be nateral, considerin' I'm your friend and her brother — you wouldn't want me standin' up in this rig. And that's puttin' it in your own point of view, Thomas."

"It strikes me," said the other, "that I could get a best man that would furnish his own clothes; but we will see about that. There's another thing, Asaph," he said, abruptly; "what are Mrs. Himes's views concernin' pipes?"

This question startled and frightened Asaph. He knew that his sister could not abide the smell of tobacco and that Mr. Rooper was an inveterate smoker.

"That depends," said he, "on the kind of tobacco. I don't mind sayin' that Marietta isn't partial to the kind of tobacco I smoke. But I ain't a moneyed man and I can't afford to buy nothin' but cheap stuff. But when it comes to a meerschaum pipe and the very finest Virginia or North Carolina smoking-tobacco, such as a moneyed man would be likely to use—"

At this moment there came from the house the sound of a woman's voice, not loud, but clear and distinct, and it said "Asaph."

This word sent through Mr. Rooper a gentle thrill such as he did not remember ever having felt before. There seemed to be in it a suggestion, a sort of prophecy, of what appeared to him as an undefined and chaotic bliss. He was not a fanciful man, but he could not help imagining himself standing alone under that chestnut-tree and that voice calling "Thomas."

Upon Asaph the effect was different. The interruption was an agreeable one in one way, because it cut short his attempted explanation of the tobacco question; but in another way he knew that it meant the swinging of an axe, and that was not pleasant.

Mr. Rooper walked back to the tavern in a

cogitative state of mind. " That Asaph Scantle," he said to himself, " has got a head-piece, there's no denying it. If it had not been for him I do not believe I should have thought of his sister; at least not until the McJimseys had left my house, and then it might have been too late."

Marietta Himes was a woman with a gentle voice and an appearance and demeanor indicative of a general softness of disposition; but beneath this mild exterior there was a great deal of firmness of purpose. Asaph had not seen very much of his sister since she had grown up and married; and when he came to live with her he thought that he was going to have things pretty much his own way. But it was not long before he entirely changed his mind.

Mrs. Himes was of moderate height, pleasant countenance, and a figure inclined to plumpness. Her dark hair, in which there was not a line of gray, was brushed down smoothly on each side of her face, and her dress, while plain, was extremely neat. In fact, everything in the house and on the place was extremely neat, except Asaph.

She was in the bright little dining-room which looked out on the flower-garden, preparing the table for supper, placing every plate, dish, glass, and cup with as much care and exactness as if a civil engineer had drawn a plan on the table-cloth with places marked for the position of each article.

As she finished her work by placing a chair on each side of the table, a quiet smile, the result of a train of thought in which she had been indulging for the past half-hour, stole over her face. She passed through the kitchen, with a glance at the stove to see if the tea-kettle had begun to boil; and going out of the back door, she walked over to the shed where her brother was splitting kindling-wood.

"Asaph," said Mrs. Himes, "if I were to give you a good suit of clothes, would you promise me that you would never smoke when wearing them?"

Her brother looked at her in amazement. "Clothes!" he repeated.

"Mr. Himes was about your size," said his sister, "and he left a good many clothes, which are most of them very good and carefully packed away, so that I am sure there is not a moth-hole in any one of them. I have several times thought, Asaph, that I might give you some of his clothes; but it did seem to me a desecration to have the clothes of such a man, who was so particular and nice, filled and saturated with horrible tobacco-smoke, which he detested. But now you are getting to be so awful shabby, I do not see how I can stand it any longer. But one thing I will not do—I will not have Mr. Himes's clothes smelling of tobacco as yours do; and not only your own tobacco, but Mr. Rooper's."

" I think," said Asaph, " that you are not exactly right just there. What you smell about me is my smoke. Thomas Rooper never uses anything but the finest-scented and delicatest brands. I think that if you come to get used to his tobacco-smoke you would like it. But as to my takin' off my clothes and puttin' on a different suit every time I want to light my pipe, that's pretty hard lines, it seems to me."

" It would be a good deal easier to give up the pipe," said his sister.

" I will do that," said Asaph, " when you give up tea. But you know as well as I do that there's no use of either of us a-tryin' to change our comfortable habits at our time of life."

" I kept on hoping," said Mrs. Himes, " that you would feel yourself that you were not fit to be seen by decent people, and that you would go to work and earn at least enough money to buy yourself some clothes. But as you don't seem inclined to do that, I thought I would make you this offer. But you must understand that I will not have you smoke in Mr. Himes's clothes."

Asaph stood thinking, the head of his axe resting upon the ground, a position which suited him. He was in a little perplexity. Marietta's proposition seemed to interfere somewhat with the one he had made to Thomas Rooper. Here was a state of affairs which required most careful considera- tion. " I've been arrangin' about some clothes,"

he said, presently; "for I know very well I
need 'em; but I don't know just yet how it will
turn out."

" I hope, Asaph," said Marietta, quickly, " that
you are not thinking of going into debt for cloth-
ing, and I know that you haven't been working
to earn money. What arrangements have you
been making? "

" That's my private affair," said Asaph, " but
there's no debt in it. It is all fair and square —
cash down, so to speak; though, of course, it's
not cash, but work. But, as I said before, that
isn't settled."

" I am afraid, Asaph," said his sister, " that if
you have to do the work first you will never get
the clothes, and so you might as well come back
to my offer."

Asaph came back to it and thought about it
very earnestly. If by any chance he could get
two suits of clothes, he would then feel that he
had a head worth having. " What would you
say," he said, presently, " if when I wanted to
smoke I was to put on a long duster — I guess
Mr. Himes had dusters — and a nightcap and
rubbers? I'd agree to hang the duster and the
cap in the shed here and never smoke without
putting 'em on." There was a deep purpose in
this proposition, for, enveloped in the long duster,
he might sit with Thomas Rooper under the chestnut-tree and smoke and talk and plan as long as

he pleased, and his companion would not know that he did not need a new suit of clothes.

"Nonsense," said Mrs. Himes; "you must make up your mind to act perfectly fairly, Asaph, or else say you will not accept my offer. But if you don't accept it, I can't see how you can keep on living with me."

"What do you mean by clothes, Marietta?" he asked.

"Well, I mean a complete suit, of course," said she.

"Winter or summer?"

"I hadn't thought of that," Mrs. Himes replied; "but that can be as you choose."

"Overcoat?" asked Asaph.

"Yes," said she, "and cane and umbrella, if you like, and pocket-handkerchiefs, too. I will fit you out completely, and shall be glad to have you looking like a decent man."

At the mention of the umbrella another line of perplexity showed itself upon Asaph's brow. The idea came to him that if she would add a dictionary he would strike a bargain. Thomas Rooper was certainly a very undecided and uncertain sort of man. But then there came up the thought of his pipe, and he was all at sea again. Giving up smoking was almost the same as giving up eating. "Marietta," said he, "I will think about this."

"Very well," she answered; "but it's my opinion, Asaph, that you ought not to take more than one minute to think about it. However, I will give you until to-morrow morning, and then if you decide that you don't care to look like a respectable citizen, I must have some further talk with you about our future arrangements."

" Make it to-morrow night," said Asaph. And his sister consented.

The next day Asaph was unusually brisk and active; and very soon after breakfast he walked over to the village tavern to see Mr. Rooper.

" Hello! " exclaimed that individual, surprised at his visitor's early appearance at the business centre of the village. " What's started you out? Have you come after them clothes? "

A happy thought struck Asaph. He had made this visit with the intention of feeling his way toward some decision on the important subject of his sister's proposition, and here a way seemed to be opened to him. " Thomas," said he, taking his friend aside, " I am in an awful fix. Marietta can't stand my clothes any longer. If she can't stand them she can't stand me, and when it comes to that, you can see for yourself that I can't help you."

A shade settled upon Mr. Rooper's face. During the past evening he had been thinking and puffing, and puffing and thinking, until everybody else in the tavern had gone to bed; and he had finally made up his mind that, if he could do it, he would marry Marietta Himes. He had never

been very intimate with her or her husband, but
he had been to meals in the house, and he remembered the fragrant coffee and the light, puffy,
well-baked rolls made by Marietta's own hands;
and he thought of the many differences between
living in that very good house with that gentle,
pleasant-voiced lady and his present life in the
village tavern.

And so, having determined that without delay
he would, with the advice and assistance of Asaph,
begin his courtship, it was natural that he should
feel a shock of discouragement when he heard
Asaph's announcement that his sister could not
endure him in the house any longer. To attack
that house and its owner without the friendly
offices upon which he depended was an undertak-
ing for which he was not at all prepared.

"I don't wonder at her," he said, sharply—
"not a bit. But this puts a mighty different face
on the thing what we talked about yesterday."

"It needn't," said Asaph, quietly. "The
clothes you was goin' to give me wouldn't cost a
cent more to-day than they would in a couple of
months, say; and when I've got 'em on Marietta
will be glad to have me around. Everything can
go on just as we bargained for."

Thomas shook his head. "That would be a
mighty resky piece of business," he said. "You
would be all right, but that's not sayin' that I
would; for it strikes me that your sister is

about as much a bird in the bush as any flyin'
critter."

Asaph smiled. "If the bush was in the middle of a field," said he, "and there was only one
boy after the bird, it would be a pretty tough job.
But if the bush is in the corner of two high walls,
and there's two boys, and one of 'em's got a fish-
net what he can throw clean over the bush, why,
then the chances is a good deal better. But
droppin' figgers, Thomas, and speakin' plain and
straightforward, as I always do —"

"About things you want to git," interrupted
Thomas.

"— about everything," resumed Asaph. "I'll
just tell you this: if I don't git decent clothes
now to-day, or perhaps to-morrow, I have got to
travel out of Marietta's house. I can do it and
she knows it. I can go back to Drummondville
and git my board for keepin' books in the store,
and nobody there cares what sort of clothes I
wear. But when that happens, your chance of
gittin' Marietta goes up higher than a kite."

To the mind of Mr. Rooper this was most con-
clusive reasoning; but he would not admit it and
he did not like it. "Why don't your sister give
you clothes?" he said. "Old Himes must have
left some."

A thin chill like a needleful of frozen thread ran
down Asaph's back. "Mr. Himes's clothes!" he
exclaimed. "What in the world are you talkin'

about, Thomas Rooper? 'Tain't likely he had
many, 'cept what he was buried in ; and what's left,
if there is any, Marietta would no more think of
givin' away than she would of hangin' up his
funeral wreath for the canary-bird to perch on.
There's a room up in the garret where she keeps
his special things — for she's awful particular —
and if there is any of his clothes up there I expect
she's got 'em framed."

"If she thinks as much of him as that," muttered Mr. Rooper.

"Now don't git any sech ideas as them into your
head, Thomas," said Asaph, quickly. "Marietta
ain't a woman to rake up the past, and you never
need be afraid of her rakin' up Mr. Himes. All
of the premises will be hern and yourn except that
room in the garret, and it ain't likely she'll ever
ask you to go in there."

"The Lord knows I don't want to!" ejaculated
Mr. Rooper.

The two men walked slowly to the end of a
line of well-used, or, rather, badly used, wooden
arm-chairs which stood upon the tavern piazza,
and seated themselves. Mr. Rooper's mind was
in a highly perturbed condition. If he accepted
Asaph's present proposition he would have to
make a considerable outlay with a very shadowy
prospect of return.

"If you haven't got the ready money for the
clothes," said Asaph, after having given his com-

panion some minutes for silent consideration,
"there ain't a man in this village what they
would trust sooner at the store for clothes," and
then after a pause he added, " or books, which,
of course, they can order from town."

At this Mr. Rooper simply shrugged his shoulders. The question of ready money or credit did
not trouble him.

At this moment a man in a low phaeton, drawn
by a stout gray horse, passed the tavern.

" Who's that? " asked Asaph, who knew everybody in the village.

" That's Doctor Wicker," said Thomas. " He
lives over at Timberley. He 'tended John Himes
in his last sickness."

" He don't practise here, does he? " said Asaph.
" J never see him."

" No; but he was called in to consult." And
then the speaker dropped again into cogitation.

After a few minutes Asaph rose. He knew that
Thomas Rooper had a slow-working mind, and
thought it would be well to leave him to himself
for a while. " I'll go home," said he, " and 'tend
to my chores, and by the time you feel like comin'
up and takin' a smoke with me under the chestnut-
tree, I reckon you will have made up your mind,
and we'll settle this thing. Fer if I have got to go
back to Drummondville, I s'pose I'll have to pack
up this afternoon."

" If you'd say pack off instead of pack up," remarked the other, " you'd come nearer the facts, considerin' the amount of your personal property. But I'll be up there in an hour or two."

When Asaph came within sight of his sister's house he was amazed to see a phaeton and a gray horse standing in front of the gate. From this it was easy to infer that the doctor was in the house. What on earth could have happened? Was anything the matter with Marietta? And if so, why did she send for a physician who lived at a distance, instead of Doctor McIlvaine, the village doctor? In a very anxious state of mind Asaph reached the gate, and irresolutely went into the yard. His impulse was to go to the house and see what had happened; but he hesitated. He felt that Marietta might object to having a comparative stranger know that such an exceedingly shabby fellow was her brother. And, besides, his sister could not have been overtaken by any sudden illness. She had always appeared perfectly well, and there would have been no time during his brief absence from the house to send over to Timberley for a doctor.

So he sat down under the chestnut-tree to consider this strange condition of affairs. " Whatever it is," he said to himself, " it's nothin' suddint, and it's bound to be chronic, and that'll skeer Thomas. I wish I hadn't asked him to come up here. The best thing for me to do will be to pretend that I have been sent to git somethin' at the store, and go straight back and keep him from comin' up."

But Asaph was a good deal quicker to think than to move, and he still sat with brows wrinkled and mind beset by doubts. For a moment he thought that it might be well to accept Marietta's proposition and let Thomas go; but then he remembered the conditions, and he shut his mental eyes at the prospect.

At that moment the gate opened and in walked Thomas Rooper. He had made up his mind and had come to say so; but the sight of the phaeton and gray horse caused him to postpone his intended announcement. "What's Doctor Wicker doin' here?" he asked, abruptly.

"Dunno," said Asaph, as carelessly as he could speak. "I don't meddle with household matters of that kind. I expect it's somethin' the matter with that gal Betsey, that Marietta hires to help her. She's always wrong some way or other so that she can't do her own proper work, which I know, havin' to do a good deal of it myself. I expect it's rickets, like as not. Gals do have that sort of thing, don't they?"

"Never had anything to do with sick gals," said Thomas, "or sick people of any sort, and don't want to. But it must be somethin' pretty deep-seated for your sister to send all the way to Timberley for a doctor."

Asaph knew very well that Mrs. Himes was

too economical a person to think of doing such a thing as that, and he knew also that Betsey was as good a specimen of rustic health as could be found in the county. And therefore his companion's statement that he wanted to have nothing to do with sick people had for him a saddening import.

"I settled that business of yourn," said Mr. Rooper, "pretty soon after you left me. I thought I might as well come straight around and tell you about it. I'll make you a fair and square offer. I'll give you them clothes, though it strikes me that winter goods will be pretty heavy for this time of year; but it will be on this condition: if I don't get Marietta, you have got to give 'em back."

Asaph smiled.

"I know what you are grinnin' at," said Thomas; "but you needn't think that you are goin' to have the wearin' of them clothes for two or three months and then give 'em back. I don't go in for any long courtships. What I do in that line will be short and sharp."

"How short?" asked Asaph.

"Well, this is Thursday," replied the other, "and I calculate to ask her on Monday."

Asaph looked at his companion in amazement. "By George!" he exclaimed, "that won't work. Why, it took Marietta more'n five days to make up her mind whether she would have the chicken-house painted green or red, and you can't expect

her to be quicker than that in takin' a new husband. She'd say No just as certain as she would
now if you was to go in and ask her right before
the doctor and Betsey. And I'll just tell you
plain that it wouldn't pay me to do all the hustlin'
around and talkin' and argyin' and recommendin'
that I'd have to do just for the pleasure of wearin'
a suit of warm clothes for four July days. I tell
you what it is, it won't do to spring that sort of
thing on a woman, especially when she's what you
might call a trained widder. You got to give
'em time to think over the matter and to look up
your references. There's no use talkin' about it;
you must give 'em time, especially when the offer
comes from a person that nobody but me has ever
thought of as a marryin' man."

"Humph!" said Thomas. "That's all you
know about it."

"Facts is facts, and you can't git around 'em.
There isn't a woman in this village what wouldn't
take at least two weeks to git it into her head
that you was really courtin' her. She would be
just as likely to think that you was tryin' to git a
tenant in place of the McJimseys. But a month
of your courtin' and a month of my workin' would
just about make the matter all right with Marietta,
and then you could sail in and settle it."

"Very good," said Mr. Rooper, rising suddenly. "I will court your sister for one month;
and if, on the 17th day of August, she takes me,

you can go up to the store and git them clothes; but you can't do it one minute afore. Good-mornin'."

Asaph, left alone, heaved a sigh. He did not despair; but truly, fate was heaping a great many obstacles in his path. He thought it was a very hard thing·for a man to get his rights in this world.

Mrs. Himes sat on one end of a black hair-covered sofa in the parlor, and Doctor Wicker sat on a black hair-covered chair opposite to her and not far away. The blinds of the window opening upon the garden were drawn up; but those on the front window, which commanded a view of the chestnut-tree, were down. Doctor Wicker had just made a proposal of marriage to Mrs. Himes, and at that moment they were both sitting in silence.

The doctor, a bluff, hearty-looking man of about forty-five, had been very favorably impressed by Mrs. Himes when he first made her acquaintance, during her husband's sickness, and since that time he had seen her occasionally and had thought about her a great deal. Latterly letters had passed be-tween them, and now he had come to make his declaration in person.

It was true, as her brother had said, that Mari-etta was not quick in making up her mind. But in this case she was able to act more promptly than usual, because she had in a great measure

settled this matter before the arrival of the doctor.
She knew he was going to propose, and she was
very much inclined to accept him. This it was
which had made her smile when she was setting
the table the afternoon before, and this it was
which had prompted her to make her proposition
to her brother in regard to his better personal
appearance.

But now she was in a condition of nervous
trepidation, and made no answer. The doctor
thought this was natural enough under the circumstances, but he had no idea of the cause of it.
The cause of it was sitting under the chestnut-tree,
the bright sunlight, streaming through a break in
the branches above, illuminating and emphasizing
and exaggerating his extreme shabbiness. The
doctor had never seen Asaph, and it would have
been a great shock to Marietta's self-respect to
have him see her brother in his present aspect.

Through a crack in the blind of the front window she had seen Asaph come in and sit down, and
she had seen Mr. Rooper arrive and had noticed
his departure. And now, with an anxiety which
made her chin tremble, she sat and hoped that
Asaph would get up and go away. For she knew
that if she should say to the doctor what she was
perfectly willing to say then and there, he would
very soon depart, being a man of practical mind
and pressing business ; and that, going to the front
door with him, she would be obliged to introduce

him to a prospective brother-in-law whose appearance, she truly believed, would make him sick. For the doctor was a man, she well knew, who was quite as nice and particular about dress and personal appearance as the late Mr. Himes had been.

Doctor Wicker, aware that the lady's perturbation was increasing instead of diminishing, thought it wise not to press the matter at this moment. He felt that he had been, perhaps, a little over-prompt in making his proposition. " Madam," said he, rising, " I will not ask you to give me an answer now. I will go away and let you think about it, and will come again to-morrow."

Through the crack in the window-blind Marietta saw that Asaph was still under the tree. What could she do to delay the doctor? She did not offer to take leave of him, but stood looking upon the floor. It seemed a shame to make so good a man go all the way back to Timberley and come again next day, just because that ragged, dirty Asaph was sitting under the chestnut-tree.

The doctor moved toward the door, and as she followed him she glanced once more through the crack in the window-blind, and, to her intense delight, she saw Asaph jump up from the bench and run around to the side of the house. He had heard the doctor's footsteps in the hallway and had not wished to meet him. The unsatisfactory condition of his outward appearance had been so strongly impressed upon him of late that he had become a little sensitive in regard to it when strangers were concerned. But if he had only known that his exceedingly unattractive garments had prevented his sister from making a compact which would have totally ruined his plans in regard to her matrimonial disposition and his own advantage, he would have felt for those old clothes the respect and gratitude with which a Roman soldier regarded the shield and sword which had won him a battle.

Down the middle of the garden, at the back of the house, there ran a path, and along this path Asaph walked meditatively, with his hands in his trousers pockets. It was a discouraging place for him to walk, for the beds on each side of him were full of weeds, which he had intended to pull out as soon as he should find time for the work, but which had now grown so tall and strong that they could not be rooted up without injuring the plants, which were the legitimate occupants of the garden.

Asaph did not know it, but at this moment there was not one person in the whole world who thought kindly of him. His sister was so mortified by him that she was in tears in the house. His crony, Thomas, had gone away almost angry with him, and even Betsey, whom he had falsely accused of rickets, and who had often shown a pity for him simply because he looked so forlorn, had steeled her heart against him that morning when she found he had gone away without providing her with any fuel for the kitchen fire.

But he had not made a dozen turns up and down the path before he became aware of the feeling of Marietta. She looked out of the back door and then walked rapidly toward him. " Asaph," said she, " I hope you are considering what I said to you yesterday, for I mean to stick to my word. If you don't choose to accept my offer, I want you to go back to Drummondville early to-morrow morning. And I don't feel in the least as if I were turning you out of the house, for I have given you a chance to stay here, and have only asked you to act like a decent Christian. I will not have you here disgracing my home. When Doctor Wicker came to-day, and I looked out and saw you with that miserable little coat with the sleeves half-way up to the elbows and great holes in it which you will not let anybody patch because you are too proud to wear patches, and those wretched faded trousers, out at the knees, and which have been turned up and hemmed at the bottom so often that they are six inches above your shoes, and your whole scarecrow appearance, I was so ashamed of you that I could not keep the tears out of my eyes. To tell a respectable gentleman like Doctor Wicker that you were my brother was more than I could bear; and I was glad when I saw you get up and sneak out of the way. I hate to talk to you in this way, Asaph, but you have brought it on yourself."

Her brother looked at her a moment. "Do you want me to go away before breakfast?" he said.

"No," answered Marietta, "but immediately afterward." And in her mind she resolved that breakfast should be very early the next morning.

If Asaph had any idea of yielding, he did not intend to show it until the last moment, and so he changed the subject. "What's the matter with Betsey?" said he. "If she's out of health you'd better get rid of her."

"There's nothing the matter with Betsey," answered his sister. "Doctor Wicker came to see me."

"Came to see you!" exclaimed her brother. "What in the world did he do that for? You never told me that you were ailin'. Is it that sprain in your ankle?"

"Nonsense," said Marietta. "I had almost recovered from that sprain when you came here. There's nothing the matter with my ankle; the trouble is probably with my heart."

The moment she said this she regretted it, for Asaph had so good a head, and could catch meanings so quickly.

"I'm sorry to hear that, Marietta," said Asaph. "That's a good deal more serious."

"Yes," said she. And she turned and went back to the house.

Asaph continued to walk up and down the path. He had not done a stroke of work that morning, but he did not think of that. His sister's communication saddened him. He liked Marietta, and it grieved him to hear that she had anything the matter with her heart. He knew that that often happened to people who looked perfectly well, and there was no reason why he should have suspected any disorder in her. Of course, in this case, there was good reason for her sending for the very best doctor to be had. It was all plain enough to him now.

But as he walked and walked and walked, and looked at the garden, and looked at the little orchard, and looked at the house and the top of the big chestnut-tree, which showed itself above the roof, a thought came into his mind which had never been there before—he was Marietta's heir. It was a dreadful thing to think of his sister's possible early departure from this world; but, after all, life is life, reality is reality, and business is business. He was Marietta's only legal heir.

Of course he had known this before, but it had never seemed to be of any importance. He was a good deal older than she was, and he had always looked upon her as a marrying woman. When he made his proposition to Mr. Rooper the thought of his own heirship never came into his

mind. In fact, if any one had offered him ten
dollars for said heirship, he would have asked
fifteen, and would have afterward agreed to split
the difference and take twelve and a half.

But now everything had changed. If Marietta
had anything the matter with her heart there was
no knowing when all that he saw might be his
own. No sooner had he walked and thought
long enough for his mind to fully appreciate the
altered aspects of his future than he determined
to instantly thrust out Mr. Rooper from all connection with that future. He would go and tell
him so at once.

To the dismay of Betsey, who had been watching him, expecting that he would soon stop walking about and go and saw some wood with which
to cook the dinner, he went out of the front gate
and strode rapidly into the village. He had some
trouble in finding Mr. Rooper, who had gone off
to take a walk and arrange a conversation with
which to begin his courtship of Mrs. Himes ; but
he overtook him under a tree by the side of the
creek. "Thomas," said he, "I have changed
my mind about that business between us. You
have been very hard on me, and I'm not goin' to
stand it. I can get the clothes and things I need
without makin' myself your slave and workin'
myself to death, and, perhaps, settin' my sister
agin me for life by tryin' to make her believe that
black's white, that you are the kind of husband

she ought to have, and that you hate pipes and never touch spirits. It would be a mean thing for me to do, and I won't do it. I did think you were a generous-minded man, with the right sort of feeling for them as wanted to be your friends; but I have found out that I was mistook, and I'm not goin' to sacrifice my sister to any such person. Now that's my state of mind plain and square."

Thomas Rooper shrunk two inches in height. "Asaph Scantle," he said, in a voice which seemed also to have shrunk, "I don't understand you. I wasn't hard on you. I only wanted to make a fair bargain. If I'd got her, I'd paid up cash on delivery. You couldn't expect a man to do more than that. But I tell you, Asaph, that I am mighty serious about this. The more I have thought about your sister the more I want her. And when I tell you that I've been a-thinkin' about her pretty much all night, you may know that I want her a good deal. And I was intendin' to go to-morrow and begin to court her."

"Well, you needn't," said Asaph. "It won't do no good. If you don't have me to back you up you might as well try to twist that tree as to move her. You can't do it."

"But you don't mean to go agin me, do you, Asaph?" asked Thomas, ruefully.

"'Tain't necessary," replied the other. "You will go agin yourself."

For a few moments Mr. Rooper remained silent.
He was greatly discouraged and dismayed by what
had been said to him, but he could not yet give
up what had become the great object of his life.
" Asaph," said he, presently, " it cuts me to the
in'ards to think that you have gone back on me;
but I tell you what I'll do: if you will promise
not to say anything agin me to Mrs. Himes, and
not to set yourself in any way between me and
her, I'll go along with you to the store now, and
you can git that suit of clothes and the umbrella,
and I'll tell 'em to order the dictionary and hand
it over to you as soon as it comes. I'd like you
to help me, but if you will only promise to stand
out of the way and not hinder, I'll do the fair
thing by you and pay in advance."

" Humph! " said Asaph. " I do believe you
think you are the only man that wants Marietta."

A pang passed through the heart of Mr. Rooper.
He had been thinking a great deal of Mrs. Himes
and everything connected with her, and he had
even thought of that visit of Doctor Wicker's.
That gentleman was a widower and a well-to-do
and well-appearing man; and it would have been
a long way for him to come just for some trifling
rickets in a servant-girl. Being really in love, his
imagination was in a very capering mood, and he
began to fear that the doctor had come to court
Mrs. Himes. " Asaph," he said, quickly, " that's
a good offer I make you. If you take it, in less

than an hour you can walk home looking like a gentleman."

Asaph had taken his reed pipe from his coat pocket and was filling it. As he pushed the coarse tobacco into the bowl, he considered. " Thomas," said he, " that ain't enough. Things have changed, and it wouldn't pay me. But I won't be hard on you. I'm a good friend of yourn, and I'll tell you what I'll do. If you will give me now all the things we spoke of between us — and I forgot to mention a cane and pocket-handkerchiefs — and give me, besides, that meer-schaum pipe of yourn, I'll promise not to hinder you, but let you go ahead and git Marietta if you kin. I must say it's a good deal for me to do, knowin' how much you'll git and how little you'll give, and knowin', too, the other chances she's got if she wanted 'em; but I'll do it for the sake of friendship."

" My meerschaum pipe!" groaned Mr. Rooper. " My Centennial Exhibition pipe! " His tones were so plaintive that for a moment Asaph felt a little touch of remorse. But then he reflected that if Thomas really did get Marietta the pipe would be of no use to him, for she would not allow him to smoke it. And, besides, realities were realities and business was business. " That pipe may be very dear to you," he said, " Thomas, but I want you to remember that Marietta's very dear to me."

This touched Mr. Rooper, whose heart was sensitive as it had never been before. "Come along, Asaph," he said. "You shall have everything, meerschaum pipe included. If anybody but me is goin' to smoke that pipe, I'd like it to be my brother-in-law." Thus, with amber-tipped guile, Mr. Rooper hoped to win over his friend to not only not hinder, but to help him.

As the two men walked away, Asaph thought that he was not acting an unfraternal part toward Marietta, for it would not be necessary for him to say or do anything to induce her to refuse so unsuitable a suitor as Thomas Rooper.

About fifteen minutes before dinner—which had been cooked with bits of wood which Betsey had picked up here and there—was ready, Asaph walked into the front yard of his sister's house attired in a complete suit of new clothes, thick and substantial in texture, pepper-and-salt in color, and as long in the legs and arms as the most fastidious could desire. He had on a new shirt and a clean collar, with a handsome black silk cravat tied in a great bow; and a new felt hat was on his head. On his left arm he carried an overcoat, carefully folded, with the lining outside, and in his right hand an umbrella and a cane. In his pockets were half a dozen new handkerchiefs and the case containing Mr. Rooper's Centennial meerschaum.

Marietta, who was in the hallway when he

opened the front door, scarcely knew him as he approached.

"Asaph!" she exclaimed. "What has happened to you? Why, you actually look like a gentleman!"

Asaph grinned. "Do you want me to go to Drummondville right after breakfast to-morrow?" he asked.

"My dear brother," said Marietta, "don't crush me by talking about that. But if you could have seen yourself as I saw you, and could have felt as I felt, you would not wonder at me. You must forget all that. I should be proud now to introduce you as my brother to any doctor or king or president. But tell me how you got those beautiful clothes."

Asaph was sometimes beset by an absurd regard for truth, which much annoyed him. He could not say that he had worked for the clothes, and he did not wish his sister to think that he had run in debt for them. "They're paid for, every thread of 'em," he said. "I got 'em in trade. These things is mine, and I don't owe no man a cent for 'em; and it seems to me that dinner must be ready."

"And proud I am," said Marietta, who never before had shown such enthusiastic affection for her brother, "to sit down to the table with such a nice-looking fellow as you are."

The next morning Mr. Rooper came into Mrs.

Himes's yard, and there beheld Asaph, in all the glory of his new clothes, sitting under the chestnut-tree smoking the Centennial meerschaum pipe. Mr. Rooper himself was dressed in his very best clothes, but he carried with him no pipe.

" Sit down," said Asaph, " and have a smoke."

" No," replied the other; " I am goin' in the house. I have come to see your sister."

" Goin' to begin already? " said Asaph.

" Yes," said the other; " I told you I was goin' to begin to-day."

" Very good," said his friend, crossing his pepper-and-salt legs; " and you will finish the 17th of August. That's a good, reasonable time."

But Mr. Rooper had no intention of courting Mrs. Himes for a month. He intended to propose to her that very morning. He had been turning over the matter in his mind, and for several reasons had come to this conclusion. In the first place, he did not believe that he could trust Asaph, even for a single day, not to oppose him. Furthermore, his mind was in such a turmoil from the combined effect of the constantly present thought that Asaph was wearing his clothes, his hat, and his shoes, and smoking his beloved pipe, and of the perplexities and agitations consequent upon his sentiments toward Mrs. Himes, that he did not believe he could bear the mental strain during another night.

Five minutes later Marietta Himes was sitting

on the horsehair sofa in the parlor, with Mr. Rooper on the horsehair chair opposite to her, and not very far away, and he was delivering the address which he had prepared.

"Madam," said he, "I am a man that takes things in this world as they comes, and is content to wait until the time comes for them to come. I was well acquainted with John Himes. I knowed him in life, and I helped lay him out. As long as there was reason to suppose that the late Mr. Himes—I mean that the grass over the grave of Mr. Himes had remained unwithered, I am not the man to take one step in the direction of his shoes, nor even to consider the size of 'em in connection with the measure of my own feet. But time will pass on in nater as well as in real life; and while I know very well, Mrs. Himes, that certain feelin's toward them that was is like the leaves of the oak-tree and can't be blowed off even by the fiercest tempests of affliction, still them leaves will wither in the fall and turn brown and curl up at the edges, though they don't depart, but stick on tight as wax all winter until in the springtime they is pushed off gently without knowin' it by the green leaves which come out in real life as well as nater."

When he had finished this opening Mr. Rooper breathed a little sigh of relief. He had not forgotten any of it, and it pleased him.

Marietta sat and looked at him. She had a

good sense of humor, and, while she was naturally surprised at what had been said to her, she was greatly amused by it, and really wished to hear what else Thomas Rooper had to say to her.

"Now, madam," he continued, "I am not the man to thrash a tree with a pole to knock the leaves off before their time. But when the young leaves is pushin' and the old leaves is droppin' (not to make any allusion, of course, to any shrivellin' of proper respect), then I come forward, madam, not to take the place of anybody else, but jest as the nateral consequence of the seasons, which everybody ought to expect; even such as you, madam, which I may liken to a hemlockspruce which keeps straight on in the same general line of appearance without no reference to the fall of the year, nor winter nor summer. And so, Mrs. Himes, I come here to-day to offer to lead you agin to the altar. I have never been there myself, and there ain't no woman in the world that I'd go with but you. I'm a straightforward person, and when I've got a thing to say I say it, and now I have said it. And so I set here awaitin' your answer."

At this moment the shutters of the front window, which had been closed, were opened, and Asaph put in his head. "Look here, Thomas Rooper," he said, "these shoes is pegged. I didn't bargain for no pegged shoes; I wanted 'em sewed; everything was to be first-class."

Mr. Rooper, who had been leaning forward in his chair, his hands upon his knees, and his face glistening with his expressed feelings as brightly as the old-fashioned but shining silk hat which stood on the floor by his side, turned his head, grew red to the ears, and then sprang to his feet. " Asaph Scantle," he cried, with extended fist, " you have broke your word; you hindered."

" No, I didn't," said Asaph, sulkily; " but pegged shoes is too much for any man to stand." And he withdrew from the window, closing the shutters again.

" What does this mean? " asked Mrs. Himes, who had also risen.

" It means," said Thomas, speaking with difficulty, his indignation was so great, " that your brother is a person of tricks and meanders beyond the reach of common human calculation. I don't like to say this of a man who is more or less likely to be my brother-in-law, but I can't help sayin' it, so entirely upset am I at his goin' back on me at such a minute."

" Going back on you? " asked Mrs. Himes. " What do you mean ?   What has he promised?"

Thomas hesitated. He did not wish to interrupt his courtship by the discussion of any new question, especially this question. " If we could settle what we have been talkin' about, Mrs. Himes," he said, " and if you would give me my answer, then I could git my mind down to commoner things. But swingin' on a hook as I am, I don't know whether my head or my heels is uppermost, or what's revolvin' around me."

" Oh, I can give you your answer quickly enough," she said. " It is impossible for me to marry you, so that's all settled."

" Impossible is a big word," said Mr. Rooper. " Has anybody else got afore me? "

" I am not bound to answer that question," said Marietta, slightly coloring; " but I cannot accept you, Mr. Rooper."

" Then there's somebody else, of course," said Thomas, gazing darkly upon the floor. " And what's more, Asaph knew it; that's just as clear as daylight. That's what made him come to me yesterday and go back on his first bargain."

" Now then," said Mrs. Himes, speaking very decidedly, " I want to know what you mean by this talk about bargains."

Mr. Rooper knit his brows. " This is mighty different talk," he said, " from the kind I expected when I come here. But you have answered my question, now I'll answer yours. Asaph Scantle, no longer ago than day before yesterday, after hearin' that things wasn't goin' very well with me, recommended me to marry you, and agreed that he would do his level best, by day and by night, to help me git you, if I would give him a suit of clothes, an umbrella, and a dictionary."

At this Mrs. Himes gave a little gasp and sat
down.

"Now, I hadn't no thoughts of tradin' for a
wife," continued Thomas, "especially in woollen
goods and books; but when I considered and
turned the matter over in my mind, and thought
what a woman you was, and what a life there was
afore me if I got you, I agreed to do it. Then
he wanted pay aforehand, and that I wouldn't
agree to, not because I thought you wasn't wuth
it, but because I couldn't trust him if anybody
offered him more before I got you. But that ain't
the wust of it; yesterday he come down to see
me and went back on his bargain, and that after
I had spent the whole night thinkin' of you and
what I was goin' to say. And he put on such
high-cockalorum airs that I, bein' as soft as mush
around the heart, jest wilted and agreed to give
him everything he bargained for if he would promise not to hinder. But he wasn't satisfied with
that and wouldn't come to no terms until I'd give
him my Centennial pipe, what's been like a child
to me this many a year. And when he saw how
disgruntled I was at sich a loss, he said that my
pipe might be very dear to me, but his sister was
jest as dear to him. And then, on top of the
whole thing, he pokes his head through the shutters and hinders jest at the most ticklish moment."

"A dictionary and a pipe!" ejaculated poor
Marietta, her eyes fixed upon the floor.

" But I'm goin' to make him give 'em all back,"
exclaimed Thomas.   " They was the price of not
hinderin', and he hindered."

" He shall give them back," said Marietta,
rising, " but you must understand, Mr. Rooper,
that in no way did Asaph interfere with your
marrying me.   That was a matter with which he
did have and could have nothing to do.   And now
I wish you could get away without speaking to
him.   I do not want any quarrelling or high
words here, and I will see him and arrange the
matter better than you can do it."

" Oh, I can git away without speakin' to him,"
said Mr. Rooper, with reddened face.   And so
saying, he strode out of the house, through the
front yard, and out of the gate, without turning
his head toward Asaph, still sitting under the
tree.

" Oh, ho!" said the latter to himself; " she's
bounced him short and sharp; and it serves him
right, too, after playin' that trick on me.   Pegged
shoes, indeed! "

At this moment the word " Asaph " came from
the house in tones shriller and sharper and higher
than any in which he had ever heard it pronounced
before.   He sprang to his feet and went to the
house.   His sister took him into the parlor and
shut the door.   Her eyes were red and her face
was pale.   " Asaph," said she, " Mr. Rooper has
told me the whole of your infamous conduct.   Now

I know what you meant when you said that you were making arrangements to get clothes. You were going to sell me for them. And when you found out that I was likely to marry Doctor Wicker, you put up your price and wanted a dictionary and a pipe."

" No, Marietta," said Asaph, " the dictionary belonged to the first bargain. If you knew how I need a dictionary —"

" Be still!" she cried. " I do not want you to say a word. You have acted most shamefully toward me, and I want you to go away this very day. And before you go you must give back to Mr. Rooper everything that you got from him. I will fit you out with some of Mr. Himes's clothes and make no conditions at all, only that you shall go away. Come upstairs with me, and I will get the clothes."

The room in the garret was opened, and various garments which had belonged to the late Mr. Himes were brought out.

" This is pretty hard on me, Marietta," said Asaph, as he held up a coat, " to give up new all-wool goods for things what has been worn and is part cotton, if I am a judge."

Marietta said very little. She gave him what clothes he needed, and insisted on his putting them on, making a package of the things he had received from Mr. Rooper, and returning them to that gentleman. Asaph at first grumbled, but

he finally obeyed with a willingness which might
have excited the suspicions of Marietta had she
not been so angry.

With an enormous package wrapped in brown
paper in one hand, and a cane, an umbrella, and
a very small hand-bag in the other, Asaph approached the tavern. Mr. Rooper was sitting on
the piazza alone. He was smoking a very com-
mon-looking clay pipe and gazing intently into
the air in front of him. When his old crony
came and stood before the piazza he did not turn
his head nor his eyes.

" Thomas Rooper," said Asaph, " you have got
me into a very bad scrape. I have been turned
out of doors on account of what you said about
me. And where I am goin' I don't know, for I
can't walk to Drummondville. And what's more,
I kept my word and you didn't. I didn't hinder
you; for how could I suppose that you was goin'
to pop the question the very minute you got inside the door? And that dictionary you promised
I've not got."

Thomas Rooper answered not a word, but looked
steadily in front of him. " And there's another
thing," said Asaph. " What are you goin' to
allow me for that suit of clothes what I've been
wearin', what I took off in your room and left
there? "

At this Mr. Rooper sprang to his feet with
such violence that the fire danced out of the bowl

of his pipe. "What is the fare to Drummond-ville?" he cried.

Asaph reflected a moment. "Three dollars and fifty cents, includin' supper."

"I'll give you that for them clothes," said the other, and counted out the money.

Asaph took it and sighed. "You've been hard on me, Thomas," said he, "but I bear you no grudge. Good-by."

As he walked slowly toward the station Mr. Scantle stopped at the store. "Has that diction-ary come that was ordered for me?" he said; and when told that it could not be expected for several days he did not despair, for it was possible that Thomas Rooper might be so angry that he would forget to countermand the order; in that case he might yet hope to obtain the coveted book.

The package containing the Rooper winter suit was heavy, and Asaph walked slowly. He did not want to go to Drummondville, for he hated bookkeeping, and his year of leisure and good living had spoiled him for work and poor fare. In this moody state he was very glad to stop and have a little chat with Mrs. McJimsey, who was sitting at her front window.

This good lady was the principal dressmaker of the village; and by hard work and attention to business she made a very comfortable living. She was a widow, small of stature, thin of feature, very neatly dressed and pleasant to look at. Asaph

entered the little front yard, put his package on
the door-step, and stood under the window to talk
to her. Dressed in the clothes of the late Mr.
Himes, her visitor presented such a respectable
appearance that Mrs. McJimsey was not in the
least ashamed to have people see him standing
there, which she would have been a few days ago.
Indeed, she felt complimented that he should want
to stop. The conversation soon turned upon her
removal from her present abode.

"I'm awfully sorry to have to go," she said;
"for my time is up just in the middle of my busy
season, and that's goin' to throw me back dreadfully. He hasn't done right by me, that Mr.
Rooper, in lettin' things go to rack and ruin in
this way, and me payin' his rent so regular."

"That's true," said Asaph. "Thomas Rooper
is a hard man — a hard man, Mrs. McJimsey. I
can see how he would be overbearin' with a lone
woman like you, neither your son nor your daughter bein' of age yet to take your part."

"Yes, Mr. Scantle, it's very hard."

Asaph stood for a moment looking at a little bed
of zinnias by the side of the door-step. "What
you want, Mrs. McJimsey," said he, "is a man
in the house."

In an instant Mrs. McJimsey flushed pink. It
was such a strange thing for a gentleman to say
to her.

Asaph saw the flush. He had not expected

that result from his remark, but he was quick to
take advantage of it. " Mrs. McJimsey," said he,
" you are a widow, and you are imposed upon, and
you need somebody to take care of you. If you
will put that job into my hands I will do it. I
am a man what works with his head, and if you
will let me I'll work for you. To put it square,
I ask you to marry me. My sister's goin' to be
married, and I'm on the pint of goin' away; for I
could not abear to stay in her house when strangers
come into it. But if you say the word, I'll stay
here and be yours for ever and ever more."

Mrs. McJimsey said not a word, but her head
drooped and wild thoughts ran through her brain.
Thoughts not wild, but well trained and broken,
ran through Asaph's brain. The idea of going
to Drummondville and spending for the journey
thither a dollar and seventy-five cents of the money
he had received from Mr. Rooper now became
absolutely repulsive to him.

" Mrs. McJimsey," said he, " I will say more.
Not only do I ask·you to marry me, but I ask
you to do it now. The evenin' sun is settin', the
evenin' birds is singin', and it seems to me, Mrs.
McJimsey, that all nater pints to this softenin'
hour as a marryin' moment. You say your son
won't be home from his work until supper-time,
and your daughter has gone out for a walk. Come
with me to Mr. Parker's, the Methodist minister,
and let us join hands at the altar there. The

gardener and his wife is always ready to stand up as witnesses. And when your son and your daughter comes home to supper, they can find their mother here afore 'em married and settled."

"But, Mr. Scantle," exclaimed Mrs. McJimsey, "it's so suddint. What will the neighbors say?"

"As for bein' suddint, Mrs. McJimsey, I've knowed you for nearly a year, and now, bein' on the way to leave what's been my happy home, I couldn't keep the truth from you no longer. And as for the neighbors, they needn't know that we hain't been engaged for months."

"It's so queer, so very queer," said the little dressmaker. And her face flushed again, and there were tears, not at all sorrowful ones, in her eyes; and her somewhat needle-pricked left hand accidentally laid itself upon the window-sill in easy reach of any one outside.

The next morning Mr. Rooper, being of a practical way of thinking, turned his thoughts from love and resentment to the subject of his income. And he soon became convinced that it would be better to keep the McJimseys in his house, if it could be done without too great an outlay for repairs. So he walked over to his property. When he reached the house he was almost stupefied to see Asaph in a chair in the front yard, dressed in the new suit of clothes which he, Thomas Rooper, had paid for, and smoking the Centennial pipe.

" Good-morning, Mr. Rooper," said Asaph, in a loud and cheery voice. " I suppose you've come to talk to Mrs. McJimsey about the work you've got to do here to make this house fit to live in. But there ain't no Mrs. McJimsey. She's Mrs. Scantle now, and I'm your tenant. You can talk to me."

Doctor Wicker came to see Mrs. Himes in the afternoon of the day he had promised to come, and early in the autumn they were married. Since Asaph Scantle had married and settled he had not seen his sister nor spoken to her; but he determined that on so joyful an occasion as this he would show no resentment. So he attended the wedding in the village church dressed in the suit of clothes which had belonged to the late Mr. Himes.

"HIS WIFE'S DECEASED SISTER"

"HIS WIFE'S DECEASED SISTER"

IT is now five years since an event occurred which so colored my life, or rather so changed some of its original colors, that I have thought it well to write an account of it, deeming that its lessons may be of advantage to persons whose situations in life are similar to my own.

When I was quite a young man I adopted literature as a profession; and having passed through the necessary preparatory grades, I found myself, after a good many years of hard and often unremunerative work, in possession of what might be called a fair literary practice. My articles, grave, gay, practical, or fanciful, had come to be considered with a favor by the editors of the various periodicals for which I wrote, on which I found in time I could rely with a very comfortable certainty. My productions created no enthusiasm in the reading public; they gave me no great reputation or very valuable pecuniary return; but they were always accepted, and my receipts from them, at the time to which I have referred, were as regular and reliable as a salary, and quite sufficient to give me more than a comfortable support.

It was at this time I married. I had been engaged for more than a year, but had not been willing to assume the support of a wife until I felt that my pecuniary position was so assured that I could do so with full satisfaction to my own conscience. There was now no doubt in regard to this position, either in my mind or in that of my wife. I worked with great steadiness and regularity; I knew exactly where to place the productions of my pen, and could calculate, with a fair degree of accuracy, the sums I should receive for them. We were by no means rich; but we had enough, and were thoroughly satisfied and content.

Those of my readers who are married will have no difficulty in remembering the peculiar ecstasy of the first weeks of their wedded life. It is then that the flowers of this world bloom brightest; that its sun is the most genial; that its clouds are the scarcest; that its fruit is the most delicious; that the air is the most balmy; that its cigars are of the highest flavor; that the warmth and radiance of early matrimonial felicity so rarefies the intellectual atmosphere that the soul mounts higher, and enjoys a wider prospect, than ever before.

These experiences were mine. The plain claret of my mind was changed to sparkling champagne, and at the very height of its effervescence I wrote a story. The happy thought that then struck me for a tale was of a very peculiar character; and it interested me so much that I went to work at it with great delight and enthusiasm, and finished it in a comparatively short time. The title of the story was " His Wife's Deceased Sister "; and when I read it to Hypatia she was delighted with it, and at times was so affected by its pathos that her uncontrollable emotion caused a sympathetic dimness in my eyes, which prevented my seeing the words I had written. When the reading was ended, and my wife had dried her eyes, she turned to me and said, " This story will make your fortune. There has been nothing so pathetic since Lamartine's ' History of a Servant-girl.' "

As soon as possible the next day I sent my story to the editor of the periodical for which I wrote most frequently, and in which my best productions generally appeared. In a few days I had a letter from the editor, in which he praised my story as he had never before praised anything from my pen. It had interested and charmed, he said, not only himself, but all his associates in the office. Even old Gibson, who never cared to read anything until it was in proof, and who never praised anything which had not a joke in it, was induced by the example of the others to read this manuscript, and shed, as he asserted, the first tears that had come from his eyes since his final paternal castigation some forty years before. The story would appear, the editor assured me, as soon as he could possibly find room for it.

If anything could make our skies more genial, our flowers brighter, and the flavor of our fruit and cigars more delicious, it was a letter like this. And when, in a very short time, the story was published, we found that the reading public was inclined to receive it with as much sympathetic interest and favor as had been shown to it by the editors. My personal friends soon began to express enthusiastic opinions upon it. It was highly praised in many of the leading newspapers; and, altogether, it was a great literary success. I am not inclined to be vain of my writings, and, in general, my wife tells me, think too little of them; but I did feel a good deal of pride and satisfaction in the success of " His Wife's Deceased Sister." If it did not make my fortune, as my wife asserted that it would, it certainly would help me very much in my literary career.

In less than a month from the writing of this story, something very unusual and unexpected happened to me. A manuscript was returned by the editor of the periodical in which " His Wife's Deceased Sister " had appeared. " It is a good story," he wrote, " but not equal to what you

have just done. You have made a great hit;
and it would not do to interfere with the reputation you have gained by publishing anything inferior to 'His Wife's Deceased Sister,' which has
had such a deserved success."

I was so unaccustomed to having my work
thrown back on my hands that I think I must
have turned a little pale when I read the letter. I
said nothing of the matter to my wife, for it would
be foolish to drop such grains of sand as this into
the smoothly oiled machinery of our domestic
felicity; but I immediately sent the story to another editor. I am not able to express the astonishment I felt when, in the course of a week,
it was sent back to me. The tone of the note ac-
companying it indicated a somewhat injured feeling on the part of the editor. "I am reluctant,"
he said, "to decline a manuscript from you; but
you know very well that if you sent me anything
like 'His Wife's Deceased Sister' it would be
most promptly accepted."

I now felt obliged to speak of the affair to my
wife, who was quite as much surprised, though,
perhaps, not quite as much shocked, as I had
been.

"Let us read the story again," she said, "and
see what is the matter with it." When we had
finished its perusal, Hypatia remarked, "It is
quite as good as many of the stories you have
had printed, and I think it very interesting; al-

though, of course, it is not equal to ' His Wife's Deceased Sister.' "

" Of course not," said I ; " that was an inspiration that I cannot expect every day. But there must be something wrong about this last story which we do not perceive. Perhaps my recent success may have made me a little careless in writing it."

" I don't believe that," said Hypatia.

" At any rate," I continued, " I will lay it aside, and will go to work on a new one."

In due course of time I had another manuscript finished, and I sent it to my favorite periodical. It was retained some weeks, and then came back to me. " It will never do," the editor wrote, quite warmly, " for you to go backward. The demand for the number containing ' His Wife's Deceased Sister' still continues, and we do not intend to let you disappoint that great body of readers who would be so eager to see another number containing one of your stories."

I sent this manuscript to four other periodicals, and from each of them was it returned with remarks to the effect that, although it was not a bad story in itself, it was not what they would expect from the author of " His Wife's Deceased Sister."

The editor of a Western magazine wrote to me for a story to be published in a special number which he would issue for the holidays. I wrote him one of the character and length he asked for, and sent it to him. By return mail it came back to me. "I had hoped," the editor wrote, "when I asked for a story from your pen, to receive something like 'His Wife's Deceased Sister,' and I must own that I am very much disappointed."

I was so filled with anger when I read this note that I openly objurgated "His Wife's Deceased Sister." "You must excuse me," I said to my astonished wife, "for expressing myself thus in your presence; but that confounded story will be the ruin of me yet. Until it is forgotten nobody will ever take anything I write."

"And you cannot expect it ever to be forgotten," said Hypatia, with tears in her eyes.

It is needless for me to detail my literary efforts in the course of the next few months. The ideas of the editors with whom my principal business had been done, in regard to my literary ability, had been so raised by my unfortunate story of "His Wife's Deceased Sister" that I found it was of no use to send them anything of lesser merit. And as to the other journals which I tried, they evidently considered it an insult for me to send them matter inferior to that by which my reputation had lately risen. The fact was that my successful story had ruined me. My income was at end, and want actually stared me in the face; and I must admit that I did not like the expression of its countenance. It was of no use for me to try to write another story like "His Wife's Deceased Sister." I could not get married every time I began a new manuscript, and it was the exaltation of mind caused by my wedded felicity which produced that story.

"It's perfectly dreadful!" said my wife. "If I had had a sister, and she had died, I would have thought it was my fault."

"It could not be your fault," I answered, "and I do not think it was mine. I had no intention of deceiving anybody into the belief that I could do that sort of thing every time, and it ought not to be expected of me. Suppose Raphael's patrons had tried to keep him screwed up to the pitch of the Sistine Madonna, and had refused to buy anything which was not as good as that. In that case I think he would have occupied a much earlier and narrower grave than that on which Mr. Morris Moore hangs his funeral decorations."

"But, my dear," said Hypatia, who was posted on such subjects, "the Sistine Madonna was one of his latest paintings."

"Very true," said I; "but if he had married, as I did, he would have painted it earlier."

I was walking homeward one afternoon about this time, when I met Barbel—a man I had known well in my early literary career. He was now about fifty years of age, but looked older. His hair and beard were quite gray; and his clothes, which were of the same general hue, gave me the idea that they, like his hair, had originally been black. Age is very hard on a man's external appointments. Barbel had an air of having been to let for a long time, and quite out of repair. But there was a kindly gleam in his eye, and he welcomed me cordially.

"Why, what is the matter, old fellow?" said he. "I never saw you look so woebegone."

I had no reason to conceal anything from Barbel. In my younger days he had been of great use to me, and he had a right to know the state of my affairs. I laid the whole case plainly before him.

"Look here," he said, when I had finished, "come with me to my room: I have something I would like to say to you there."

I followed Barbel to his room. It was at the top of a very dirty and well-worn house ·which stood in a narrow and lumpy street, into which few vehicles ever penetrated, except the ash and garbage carts, and the rickety wagons of the venders of stale vegetables.

"This is not exactly a fashionable promenade," said Barbel, as we approached the house; "but in some respects it reminds me of the streets in Italian towns, where the palaces lean over toward each other in such a friendly way."

Barbel's room was, to my mind, rather more doleful than the street. It was dark, it was dusty, and cobwebs hung from every corner.

The few chairs upon the floor and the books upon a greasy table seemed to be afflicted with some dorsal epidemic, for their backs were either gone or broken. A little bedstead in the corner was covered with a spread made of New York *Heralds*, with their edges pasted together.

" There is nothing better," said Barbel, noticing my glance toward this novel counterpane, " for a bed-covering than newspapers : they keep you as warm as a blanket, and are much lighter. I used to use *Tribunes*, but they rattled too much."

The only part of the room which was well lighted was at one end near the solitary window. Here, upon a table with a spliced leg, stood a little grindstone.

" At the other end of the room," said Barbel, " is my cook-stove, which you can't see unless I light the candle in the bottle which stands by it ; but if you don't care particularly to examine it, I won't go to the expense of lighting up. You might pick up a good many odd pieces of bric-à-brac around here, if you chose to strike a match and investigate ; but I would not advise you to do so. It would pay better to throw the things out of the window than to carry them downstairs. The particular piece of indoor decoration to which I wish to call your attention is this." And he led me to a little wooden frame which hung against the wall near the window. Behind a dusty piece of glass it held what appeared to be a leaf from a small magazine or journal. "There," said he, " you see a page from the *Grasshopper*, a humorous paper which flourished in this city some half-dozen years ago. I used to write regularly for that paper, as you may remember."

"Oh yes, indeed!" I exclaimed. "And I shall never forget your ' Conundrum of the Anvil ' which appeared in it. How often have I laughed at that most wonderful conceit, and how often have I put it to my friends!"

Barbel gazed at me silently for a moment, and then he pointed to the frame. "That printed page," he said, solemnly, "contains the ' Conundrum of the Anvil.' I hang it there so that I can see it while I work. That conundrum ruined me. It was the last thing I wrote for the *Grasshopper*. How I ever came to imagine it I cannot tell. It is one of those things which occur to a man but once in a lifetime. After the wild shout of delight with which the public greeted that conundrum, my subsequent efforts met with hoots of derision. The *Grasshopper* turned its hind legs upon me. I sank from bad to worse — much worse — until at last I found myself reduced to my present occupation, which is that of grinding points to pins. By this I procure my bread, coffee, and tobacco, and sometimes potatoes and meat. One day while I was hard at work an organ-grinder came into the street below. He played the serenade from "Trovatore"; and the familiar notes brought

back visions of old days and old delights, when
the successful writer wore good clothes and sat at
operas, when he looked into sweet eyes and talked
of Italian airs, when his future appeared all a suc-
cession of bright scenery and joyous acts, without
any provision for a drop-curtain. And as my ear
listened, and my mind wandered in this happy
retrospect, my every faculty seemed exalted, and,
without any thought upon the matter, I ground
points upon my pins so fine, so regular and
smooth, that they would have pierced with ease
the leather of a boot, or slipped among, without
abrasion, the finest threads of rare old lace.
When the organ stopped, and I fell back into my
real world of cobwebs and mustiness, I gazed
upon the pins I had just ground, and, without a
moment's hesitation, I threw them into the street,
and reported the lot as spoiled. This cost me a
little money, but it saved me my livelihood."

After a few moments of silence, Barbel resumed :

" I have no more to say to you, my young friend.
All I want you to do is to look upon that framed
conundrum, then upon this grindstone, and then
to go home and reflect. As for me, I have a gross
of pins to grind before the sun goes down."

I cannot say that my depression of mind was at
all relieved by what I had seen and heard. I had
lost sight of Barbel for some years, and I had
supposed him still floating on the sun-sparkling

stream of prosperity where I had last seen him.
It was a great shock to me to find him in such a
condition of poverty and squalor, and to see a
man who had originated the " Conundrum of the
Anvil " reduced to the soul-depressing occupation
of grinding pin-points.   As I walked and thought,
the dreadful picture of a totally eclipsed future
arose before my mind.   The moral of Barbel sank
deep into my heart.

When I reached home I told my wife the story
of my friend Barbel.   She listened with a sad and
eager interest.

" I am afraid," she said, " if our fortunes do
not quickly mend, that we shall have to buy two
little grindstones.   You know I could help you
at that sort of thing."

For a long time we sat together and talked,
and devised many plans for the future.   I did
not think it necessary yet for me to look out for
a pin-contract; but I must find some way of making money, or we should starve to death.   Of
course the first thing that suggested itself was
the possibility of finding some other business;
but, apart from the difficulty of immediately ob-
taining remunerative work in occupations to which
I had not been trained, I felt a great and natural
reluctance to give up a profession for which I
had carefully prepared myself, and which I had
adopted as my life-work.   It would be very
hard for me to lay down my pen forever, and to

close the top of my inkstand upon all the bright and happy fancies which I had seen mirrored in its tranquil pool. We talked and pondered the rest of that day and a good deal of the night, but we came to no conclusion as to what it would be best for us to do.

The next day I determined to go and call upon the editor of the journal for which, in happier days, before the blight of " His Wife's Deceased Sister " rested upon me, I used most frequently to write, and, having frankly explained my condition to him, to ask his advice. The editor was a good man, and had always been my friend. He listened with great attention to what I told him, and evidently sympathized with me in my trouble.

" As we have written to you," he said, " the only reason why we did not accept the manuscripts you sent us was that they would have disappointed the high hopes that the public had formed in regard to you. We have had letter after letter asking when we were going to publish another story like ' His Wife's Deceased Sister.' We felt, and we still feel, that it would be wrong to allow you to destroy the fair fabric which yourself has raised. But," he added, with a kind smile, " I see very plainly that your well-deserved reputation will be of little advantage to you if you should starve at the moment that its genial beams are, so to speak, lighting you up."

" Its beams are not genial," I answered.
" They have scorched and withered me."

" How would you like," said the editor, after
a short reflection, " to allow us to publish the
stories you have recently written under some other
name than your own? That would satisfy us and
the public, would put money in your pocket, and
would not interfere with your reputation."

Joyfully I seized that noble fellow by the hand,
and instantly accepted his proposition. " Of
course," said I, " a reputation is a very good
thing; but no reputation can take the place of
food, clothes, and a house to live in; and I
gladly agree to sink my over-illumined name
into oblivion, and to appear before the public as
a new and unknown writer."

" I hope that need not be for long," he said,
" for I feel sure that you will yet write stories as
good as ' His Wife's Deceased Sister.' "

All the manuscripts I had on hand I now sent
to my good friend the editor, and in due and
proper order they appeared in his journal under
the name of John Darmstadt, which I had selected as a substitute for my own, permanently
disabled. I made a similar arrangement with
other editors, and John Darmstadt received the
credit of everything that proceeded from my pen.
Our circumstances now became very comfortable,
and occasionally we even allowed ourselves to
indulge in little dreams of prosperity.

Time passed on very pleasantly; one year, another, and then a little son was born to us. It is often difficult, I believe, for thoughtful persons to decide whether the beginning of their conjugal career, or the earliest weeks in the life of their first-born, be the happiest and proudest period of their existence. For myself I can only say that the same exaltation of mind, the same rarefication of idea and invention, which succeeded upon my wedding-day came upon me now. As then, my ecstatic emotions crystallized themselves into a motive for a story, and without delay I set myself to work upon it. My boy was about six weeks old when the manuscript was finished; and one evening, as we sat before a comfortable fire in our sitting-room, with the curtains drawn, and the soft lamp lighted, and the baby sleeping soundly in the adjoining chamber, I read the story to my wife.

When I had finished, my wife arose and threw herself into my arms. "I was never so proud of you," she said, her glad eyes sparkling, "as I am at this moment. That is a wonderful story! It is—indeed I am sure it is—just as good as 'His Wife's Deceased Sister.'"

As she spoke these words a sudden and chilling sensation crept over us both. All her warmth and fervor, and the proud and happy glow engendered within me by this praise and appreciation from one I loved, vanished in an instant. We stepped

apart, and gazed upon each other with pallid
faces. In the same moment the terrible truth
had flashed upon us both.

This story *was* as good as " His Wife's Deceased Sister "!

We stood silent. The exceptional lot of Barbel's superpointed pins seemed to pierce our very
souls. A dreadful vision rose before me of an
impending fall and crash, in which our domestic
happiness should vanish, and our prospects for
our boy be wrecked, just as we had begun to
build them up.

My wife approached me and took my hand in
hers, which was as cold as ice. " Be strong and
firm," she said. " A great danger threatens us,
but you must brace yourself against it. Be
strong and firm."

I pressed her hand, and we said no more that
night.

The next day I took the manuscript I had just
written, and carefully infolded it in stout wrap-
ping-paper. Then I went to a neighboring
grocery-store and bought a small, strong tin
box, originally intended for biscuit, with a cover
that fitted tightly. In this I placed my manuscript; and then I took the box to a tinsmith and
had the top fastened on with hard solder. When
I went home I ascended into the garret, and
brought down to my study a ship's cash-box,
which had once belonged to one of my family

who was a sea-captain. This box was very heavy, and firmly bound with iron, and was secured by two massive locks. Calling my wife, I told her of the contents of the tin case, which I then placed in the box, and, having shut down the heavy lid, I doubly locked it.

"This key," said I, putting it in my pocket, "I shall throw into the river when I go out this afternoon."

My wife watched me eagerly, with a pallid and firm, set countenance, but upon which I could see the faint glimmer of returning happiness.

"Wouldn't it be well," she said, "to secure it still further by sealing-wax and pieces of tape?"

"No," said I. "I do not believe that any one will attempt to tamper with our prosperity. And now, my dear," I continued, in an impressive voice, "no one but you, and, in the course of time, our son, shall know that this manuscript exists. When I am dead, those who survive me may, if they see fit, cause this box to be split open and the story published. The reputation it may give my name cannot harm me then."

THE LADY, OR THE TIGER?

THE LADY, OR THE TIGER?

N the very olden time there lived a semi-barbaric king, whose ideas, though somewhat polished and sharpened by the progressiveness of distant Latin neighbors, were still large, florid, and untrammelled, as became the half of him which was barbaric. He was a man of exuberant fancy, and, withal, of an authority so irresistible that, at his will, he turned his varied fancies into facts. He was greatly given to self-communing; and when he and himself agreed upon anything, the thing was done. When every member of his domestic and political systems moved smoothly in its appointed course, his nature was bland and genial; but whenever there was a little hitch, and some of his orbs got out of their orbits, he was blander and more genial still, for nothing pleased him so much as to make the crooked straight, and crush down uneven places.

Among the borrowed notions by which his bar-

barism had become semified was that of the public arena, in which, by exhibitions of manly and
beastly valor, the minds of his subjects were re-
fined and cultured.

But even here the exuberant and barbaric fancy
asserted itself.   The arena of the king was built
not to give the people an opportunity of hearing
the rhapsodies of dying gladiators, nor to enable
them to view the inevitable conclusion of a con-
flict between religious opinions and hungry jaws,
but for purposes far better adapted to widen and
develop the mental energies of the people.   This
vast amphitheatre, with its encircling galleries,
its mysterious vaults, and its unseen passages,
was an agent of poetic justice, in which crime
was punished, or virtue rewarded, by the decrees
of an impartial and incorruptible chance.

When a subject was accused of a crime of sufficient importance to interest the king, public notice
was given that on an appointed day the fate of the
accused person would be decided in the king's
arena—a structure which well deserved its name;
for, although its form and plan were borrowed
from afar, its purpose emanated solely from the
brain of this man, who, every barleycorn a king,
knew no tradition to which he owed more alle-
giance than pleased his fancy, and who ingrafted
on every adopted form of human thought and
action the rich growth of his barbaric idealism.

When all the people had assembled in the galleries, and the king, surrounded by his court, sat high up on his throne of royal state on one side of the arena, he gave a signal, a door beneath him opened, and the accused subject stepped out into the amphitheatre. Directly opposite him, on the other side of the enclosed space, were two doors, exactly alike and side by side. It was the duty and the privilege of the person on trial to walk directly to these doors and open one of them. He could open either door he pleased: he was subject to no guidance or influence but that of the afore-mentioned impartial and incorruptible chance. If he opened the one, there came out of it a hungry tiger, the fiercest and most cruel that could be procured, which immediately sprang upon him and tore him to pieces, as a punishment for his guilt. The moment that the case of the criminal was thus decided, doleful iron bells were clanged, great wails went up from the hired mourners posted on the outer rim of the arena, and the vast audience, with bowed heads and downcast hearts, wended slowly their homeward way, mourning greatly that one so young and fair, or so old and respected, should have merited so dire a fate.

But if the accused person opened the other door, there came forth from it a lady, the most suitable to his years and station that his Majesty could select among his fair subjects; and to this lady he was immediately married, as a reward of his innocence. It mattered not that he might already possess a wife and family, or that his affections might be engaged upon an object of his own selection: the king allowed no such subordinate arrangements to interfere with his great scheme of retribution and reward. The exercises, as in the other instance, took place immediately, and in the arena. Another door opened beneath the king, and a priest, followed by a band of choristers, and dancing maidens blowing joyous airs on golden horns and treading an epithalamic measure, advanced to where the pair stood side by side; and the wedding was promptly and cheerily solemnized. Then the gay brass bells rang forth their merry peals, the people shouted glad hurrahs, and the innocent man, preceded by children strewing flowers on his path, led his bride to his home.

This was the king's semibarbaric method of administering justice. Its perfect fairness is obvious. The criminal could not know out of which door would come the lady: he opened either he pleased, without having the slightest idea whether, in the next instant, he was to be devoured or married. On some occasions the tiger came out of one door, and on some out of the other. The decisions of this tribunal were not only fair, they were positively determinate: the accused person was instantly punished if he found himself guilty; and if innocent, he was rewarded on the spot, whether he liked it or not.

There was no escape from the judgments of the king's arena.

The institution was a very popular one. When the people gathered together on one of the great trial-days, they never knew whether they were to witness a bloody slaughter or a hilarious wedding. This element of uncertainty lent an interest to the occasion which it could not otherwise have attained. Thus the masses were entertained and pleased, and the thinking part of the community could bring no charge of unfairness against this plan; for did not the accused person have the whole matter in his own hands?

This semibarbaric king had a daughter as blooming as his most florid fancies, and with a soul as fervent and imperious as his own. As is usual in such cases, she was the apple of his eye, and was loved by him above all humanity. Among his courtiers was a young man of that fineness of blood and lowness of station common to the conventional heroes of romance who love royal maidens. This royal maiden was well satisfied with her lover, for he was handsome and brave to a degree unsurpassed in all this kingdom; and she loved him with an ardor that had enough of barbarism in it to make it exceedingly warm and strong. This love-affair moved on happily for many months, until one day the king happened to discover its existence. He did not hesitate nor waver in regard to his duty in the premises.

The youth was immediately cast into prison, and a day was appointed for his trial in the king's arena. This, of course, was an especially important occasion; and his Majesty, as well as all the people, was greatly interested in the workings and development of this trial. Never before had such a case occurred; never before had a subject dared to love the daughter of a king. In after-years such things became commonplace enough; but then they were, in no slight degree, novel and startling.

The tiger-cages of the kingdom were searched for the most savage and relentless beasts, from which the fiercest monster might be selected for the arena; and the ranks of maiden youth and beauty throughout the land were carefully surveyed by competent judges, in order that the young man might have a fitting bride in case fate did not determine for him a different destiny. Of course everybody knew that the deed with which the accused was charged had been done. He had loved the princess, and neither he, she, nor any one else thought of denying the fact; but the king would not think of allowing any fact of this kind to interfere with the workings of the tribunal, in which he took such great delight and satisfaction. No matter how the affair turned out, the youth would be disposed of; and the king would take an æsthetic pleasure in watching the course of events, which would determine whether or not

the young man had done wrong in allowing himself to love the princess.

The appointed day arrived. From far and
near the people gathered, and thronged the great
galleries of the arena; and crowds, unable to gain
admittance, massed themselves against its outside
walls. The king and his court were in their
places, opposite the twin doors—those fateful
portals, so terrible in their similarity.

All was ready. The signal was given. A door
beneath the royal party opened, and the lover of
the princess walked into the arena. Tall, beautiful, fair, his appearance was greeted with a low
hum of admiration and anxiety. Half the audience had not known so grand a youth had lived
among them. No wonder the princess loved him!
What a terrible thing for him to be there!

As the youth advanced into the arena, he turned,
as the custom was, to bow to the king: but he did
not think at all of that royal personage; his eyes
were fixed upon the princess, who sat to the right
of her father. Had it not been for the moiety of
barbarism in her nature it is probable that lady
would not have been there; but her intense and
fervid soul would not allow her to be absent on an
occasion in which she was so terribly interested.
From the moment that the decree had gone forth
that her lover should decide his fate in the king's
arena, she had thought of nothing, night or day,
but this great event and the various subjects con-

nected with it. Possessed of more power, influence, and force of character than any one who had
ever before been interested in such a case, she had
done what no other person had done—she had
possessed herself of the secret of the doors. She
knew in which of the two rooms that lay behind
those doors stood the cage of the tiger, with its
open front, and in which waited the lady. Through
these thick doors, heavily curtained with skins on
the inside, it was impossible that any noise or
suggestion should come from within to the person who should approach to raise the latch
of one of them; but gold, and the power of a
woman's will, had brought the secret to the
princess.

And not only did she know in which room stood
the lady ready to emerge, all blushing and radiant,
should her door be opened, but she knew who the
lady was. It was one of the fairest and loveliest
of the damsels of the court who had been selected
as the reward of the accused youth, should he be
proved innocent of the crime of aspiring to one so
far above him; and the princess hated her. Often
had she seen, or imagined that she had seen, this
fair creature throwing glances of admiration upon
the person of her lover, and sometimes she thought
these glances were perceived and even returned.
Now and then she had seen them talking together;
it was but for a moment or two, but much can be
said in a brief space; it may have been on most

unimportant topics, but how could she know that?
The girl was lovely, but she had dared to raise
her eyes to the loved one of the princess; and,
with all the intensity of the savage blood trans-
mitted to her through long lines of wholly barbaric
ancestors, she hated the woman who blushed and
trembled behind that silent door.

When her lover turned and looked at her, and
his eye met hers as she sat there paler and whiter
than any one in the vast ocean of anxious faces
about her, he saw, by that power of quick percep-
tion which is given to those whose souls are one,
that she knew behind which door crouched the
tiger, and behind which stood the lady. He had
expected her to know it. He understood her nature, and his soul was assured that she would never
rest until she had made plain to herself this thing,
hidden to all other lookers-on, even to the king.
The only hope for the youth in which there was
any element of certainty was based upon the success of the princess in discovering this mystery;
and the moment he looked upon her, he saw she
had succeeded, as in his soul he knew she would
succeed.

Then it was that his quick and anxious glance
asked the question, "Which?" It was as plain
to her as if he shouted it from where he stood.
There was not an instant to be lost. The question was asked in a flash; it must be answered in
another.

Her right arm lay on the cushioned parapet before her.   She raised her hand, and made a slight,
quick movement toward the right.   No one but
her lover saw her.   Every eye but his was fixed
on the man in the arena.

He turned, and with a firm and rapid step he
walked across the empty space.   Every heart
stopped beating, every breath was held, every
eye was fixed immovably upon that man.   Without the slightest hesitation, he went to the door
on the right, and opened it.

Now, the point of the story is this: Did the
tiger come out of that door, or did the lady?

The more we reflect upon this question the
harder it is to answer.   It involves a study of
the human heart which leads us through devious
mazes of passion, out of which it is difficult to
find our way.   Think of it, fair reader, not as if
the decision of the question depended upon yourself, but upon that hot-blooded, semibarbaric princess, her soul at a white heat beneath the combined
fires of despair and jealousy.   She had lost him,
but who should have him?

How often, in her waking hours and in her
dreams, had she started in wild horror and covered her face with her hands as she thought of
her lover opening the door on the other side of
which waited the cruel fangs of the tiger!

But how much oftener had she seen him at the

other door! How in her grievous reveries had
she gnashed her teeth and torn her hair when she
saw his start of rapturous delight as he opened the
door of the lady! How her soul had burned in
agony when she had seen him rush to meet that
woman, with her flushing cheek and sparkling
eye of triumph; when she had seen him lead her
forth, his whole frame kindled with the joy of recovered life; when she had heard the glad shouts
from the multitude, and the wild ringing of the
happy bells; when she had seen the priest, with
his joyous followers, advance to the couple, and
make them man and wife before her very eyes;
and when she had seen them walk away together
upon their path of flowers, followed by the tre-
mendous shouts of the hilarious multitude, in
which her one despairing shriek was lost and
drowned!

Would it not be better for him to die at once,
and go to wait for her in the blessed regions of
semibarbaric futurity?

And yet, that awful tiger, those shrieks, that
blood!

Her decision had been indicated in an instant,
but it had been made after days and nights of
anguished deliberation. She had known she
would be asked, she had decided what she would
answer, and, without the slightest hesitation, she
had moved her hand to the right.

The question of her decision is one not to be

lightly considered, and it is not for me to presume
to set myself up as the one person able to answer
it.   And so I leave it with all of you: Which
came out of the opened door—the lady, or the
tiger?

THE REMARKABLE WRECK OF
THE "THOMAS HYKE"

THE REMARKABLE WRECK OF
THE "THOMAS HYKE"

IT was half-past one by the clock in the office of the Registrar of Woes. The room was empty, for it was Wednesday, and the Registrar always went home early on Wednesday afternoons. He had made that arrangement when he accepted the office. He was willing to serve his fellow-citizens in any suitable position to which he might be called, but he had private interests which could not be neglected. He belonged to his country, but there was a house in the country which belonged to him; and there were a great many things appertaining to that house which needed attention, especially in pleasant summer weather. It is true he was often absent on afternoons which did not fall on the Wednesday, but the fact of his having appointed a particular time for the furtherance of his outside interests so em-

phasized their importance that his associates in
the office had no difficulty in understanding that
affairs of such moment could not always be attended to in a single afternoon of the week.

But although the large room devoted to the
especial use of the Registrar was unoccupied,
there were other rooms connected with it which
were not in that condition. With the suite of
offices to the left we have nothing to do, but will
confine our attention to a moderate-sized room to
the right of the Registrar's office, and connected
by a door, now closed, with that large and handsomely furnished chamber. This was the office
of the Clerk of Shipwrecks, and it was at present
occupied by five persons. One of these was the
clerk himself, a man of goodly appearance, somewhere between twenty-five and forty-five years of
age, and of a demeanor such as might be supposed
to belong to one who had occupied a high position in state affairs, but who, by the cabals of his
enemies, had been forced to resign the great opera-
tions of statesmanship which he had been direct-
ing, and who now stood, with a quite resigned air,
pointing out to the populace the futile and dis-
astrous efforts of the incompetent one who was
endeavoring to fill his place. The Clerk of Shipwrecks had never fallen from such a position,
having never occupied one, but he had acquired
the demeanor referred to without going through
the preliminary exercises.

Another occupant was a very young man, the personal clerk of the Registrar of Woes, who always closed all the doors of the office of that functionary on Wednesday afternoons, and at other times when outside interests demanded his principal's absence, after which he betook himself to the room of his friend the Shipwreck Clerk.

Then there was a middle-aged man named Mathers, also a friend of the clerk, and who was one of the eight who had made application for a subposition in this department, which was now filled by a man who was expected to resign when a friend of his, a gentleman of influence in an interior county, should succeed in procuring the nomination as congressional Representative of his district of an influential politician, whose election was considered assured in case certain expected action on the part of the administration should bring his party into power. The person now occupying the subposition hoped then to get something better, and Mathers, consequently, was very willing, while waiting for the place, to visit the offices of the department and acquaint himself with its duties.

A fourth person was J. George Watts, a juryman by profession, who had brought with him his brother-in-law, a stranger in the city.

The Shipwreck Clerk had taken off his good coat, which he had worn to luncheon, and had replaced it by a lighter garment of linen, much bespattered with ink; and he now produced a cigar-box, containing six cigars.

"Gents," said he, "here is the fag end of a box of cigars. It's not like having the pick of a box, but they are all I have left."

Mr. Mathers, J. George Watts, and the brother-in-law each took a cigar with that careless yet deferential manner which always distinguishes the treatee from the treator; and then the box was protruded in an offhand way toward Harry Covare, the personal clerk of the Registrar; but this young man declined, saying that he preferred cigarettes, a package of which he drew from his pocket. He had very often seen that cigar-box with a Havana brand, which he himself had brought from the other room after the Registrar had emptied it, passed around with six cigars, no more nor less, and he was wise enough to know that the Shipwreck Clerk did not expect to supply him with smoking-material. If that gentleman had offered to the friends who generally dropped in on him on Wednesday afternoon the paper bag of cigars sold at five cents each when bought singly, but half a dozen for a quarter of a dollar, they would have been quite as thankfully received; but it better pleased his deprecative soul to put them in an empty cigar-box, and thus throw around them the halo of the presumption that ninety-four of their imported companions had been smoked.

The Shipwreck Clerk, having lighted a cigar for himself, sat down in his revolving chair, turned his back to his desk, and threw himself into an easy cross-legged attitude, which showed that he was perfectly at home in that office. Harry Covare mounted a high stool, while the visitors seated themselves in three wooden arm-chairs. But few words had been said, and each man had scarcely tossed his first tobacco-ashes on the floor, when some one wearing heavy boots was heard opening an outside door and entering the Registrar's room. Harry Covare jumped down from his stool, laid his half-smoked cigarette thereon, and bounced into the next room, closing the door after him. In about a minute he returned, and the Shipwreck Clerk looked at him inquiringly.

"An old cock in a pea-jacket," said Mr. Covare, taking up his cigarette and mounting his stool. "I told him the Registrar would be here in the morning. He said he had something to report about a shipwreck, and I told him the Registrar would be here in the morning. Had to tell him that three times, and then he went."

"School don't keep Wednesday afternoons," said Mr. J. George Watts, with a knowing smile.

"No, sir," said the Shipwreck Clerk, emphatically, changing the crossing of his legs. "A man can't keep grinding on day in and out without breaking down. Outsiders may say what they please about it, but it can't be done. We've got to let up sometimes. People who do the work need the rest just as much as those who do the looking on."

" And more too, I should say," observed Mr. Mathers.

" Our little let-up on Wednesday afternoons," modestly observed Harry Covare, " is like death —it is sure to come; while the let-ups we get other days are more like the diseases which prevail in certain areas—you can't be sure whether you're going to get them or not."

The Shipwreck Clerk smiled benignantly at this remark, and the rest laughed. Mr. Mathers had heard it before, but he would not impair the pleasantness of his relations with a future colleague by hinting that he remembered it.

" He gets such ideas from his beastly statistics," said the Shipwreck Clerk.

" Which come pretty heavy on him sometimes, I expect," observed Mr. Mathers.

" They needn't," said the Shipwreck Clerk, " if things were managed here as they ought to be.   If John J. Laylor "—meaning thereby the Registrar—" was the right kind of a man you'd see things very different here from what they are now.   There'd be a larger force."

" That's so," said Mr. Mathers.

" And not only that, but there'd be better buildings and more accommodations.   Were any of you ever up to Anster? Well, take a run up there some day, and see what sort of buildings the department has there. William Q. Green is a very different man from John J. Laylor. You don't see him sitting in his chair and picking his teeth the whole winter, while the Representative from his district never says a word about his department from one end of a session of Congress to the other. Now if I had charge of things here, I'd make such changes that you wouldn't know the place. I'd throw two rooms off here, and a corridor and entrance-door at that end of the building. I'd close up this door "—pointing toward the Registrar's room—" and if John J. Laylor wanted to come in here he might go round to the end door like other people."

The thought struck Harry Covare that in that case there would be no John J. Laylor, but he would not interrupt.

" And what is more," continued the Shipwreck Clerk, " I'd close up this whole department at twelve o'clock on Saturdays. The way things are managed now, a man has no time to attend to his own private business. Suppose I think of buying a piece of land, and want to go out and look at it, or suppose any one of you gentlemen were here and thought of buying a piece of land and wanted to go out and look at it, what are you going to do about it? You don't want to go on Sunday, and when are you going to go?"

Not one of the other gentlemen had ever
thought of buying a piece of land, nor had they
any reason to suppose that they ever would purchase an inch of soil unless they bought it in
a flower-pot; but they all agreed that the way
things were managed now there was no time for
a man to attend to his own business.

"But you can't expect John J. Laylor to do
anything," said the Shipwreck Clerk.

However, there was one thing which that
gentleman always expected John J. Laylor to do.
When the clerk was surrounded by a number of
persons in hours of business, and when he had
succeeded in impressing them with the importance of his functions and the necessity of paying
deferential attention to himself if they wished their
business attended to, John J. Laylor would be sure
to walk into the office and address the Shipwreck
Clerk in such a manner as to let the people present know that he was a clerk and nothing else,
and that he, the Registrar, was the head of that
department. These humiliations the Shipwreck
Clerk never forgot.

There was a little pause here, and then Mr.
Mathers remarked:

"I should think you'd be awfully bored with
the long stories of shipwrecks that the people
come and tell you."

He hoped to change the conversation, because,
although he wished to remain on good terms with

the subordinate officers, it was not desirable that he should be led to say much against John J. Laylor.

" No, sir," said the Shipwreck Clerk, " I am not bored. I did not come here to be bored, and as long as I have charge of this office I don't intend to be. The long-winded old salts who come here to report their wrecks never spin out their prosy yarns to me. The first thing I do is to let them know just what I want of them; and not an inch beyond that does a man of them go, at least while I am managing the business. There are times when John J. Laylor comes in, and puts in his oar, and wants to hear the whole story; which is pure stuff and nonsense, for John J. Laylor doesn't know anything more about a shipwreck than he does about—"

" The endemies in the Lake George area," suggested Harry Covare.

" Yes; or any other part of his business," said the Shipwreck Clerk; " and when he takes it into his head to interfere, all business stops till some second mate of a coal-schooner has told his whole story from his sighting land on the morning of one day to his getting ashore on it on the afternoon of the next. Now I don't put up with any such nonsense. There's no man living that can tell me anything about shipwrecks. I've never been to sea myself, but that's not necessary; and if I had gone, it's not likely I'd been wrecked. But I've read about every kind of shipwreck that

ever happened. When I first came here I took
care to post myself upon these matters, because
I knew it would save trouble. I have read
' Robinson Crusoe,' ' The Wreck of the " Grosve-
nor," ' ' The Sinking of the " Royal George," ' and
wrecks by water-spouts, tidal waves, and every
other thing which would knock a ship into a
cocked hat, and I've classified every sort of wreck
under its proper head; and when I've found out
to what class a wreck belongs, I know all about it.
Now, when a man comes here to report a wreck,
the first thing he has to do is just to shut down on
his story, and to stand up square and answer a
few questions that I put to him. In two minutes
I know just what kind of shipwreck he's had;
and then, when he gives me the name of his
vessel, and one or two other points, he may go.
I know all about that wreck, and I make a much
better report of the business than he could have
done if he'd stood here talking three days and
three nights. The amount of money that's been
saved to our taxpayers by the way I've systema-
tized the business of this office is not to be calcu-
lated in figures."

The brother-in-law of J. George Watts knocked
the ashes from the remnant of his cigar, looked
contemplatively at the coal for a moment, and
then remarked:

" I think you said there's no kind of shipwreck
you don't know about? "

" That's what I said," replied the Shipwreck Clerk.

" I think," said the other, " I could tell you of a shipwreck, in which I was concerned, that wouldn't go into any of your classes."

The Shipwreck Clerk threw away the end of his cigar, put both his hands into his trousers pockets, stretched out his legs, and looked steadfastly at the man who had made this unwarrantable remark. Then a pitying smile stole over his countenance, and he said: " Well, sir, I'd like to hear your account of it; and before you get a quarter through I can stop you just where you are, and go ahead and tell the rest of the story myself."

" That's so," said Harry Covarc. " You'll see him do it just as sure pop as a spread rail bounces the engine."

" Well, then," said the brother-in-law of J. George Watts, " I'll tell it." And he began:

" It was just two years ago the 1st of this month that I sailed for South America in the ' Thomas Hyke.' "

At this point the Shipwreck Clerk turned and opened a large book at the letter T.

" That wreck wasn't reported here," said the other, " and you won't find it in your book."

" At Anster, perhaps?" said the Shipwreck Clerk, closing the volume and turning round again.

" Can't say about that," replied the other.
" I've never been to Anster, and haven't looked
over their books."

" Well, you needn't want to," said the clerk.
" They've got good accommodations at Anster,
and the Registrar has some ideas of the duties of
his post, but they have no such system of wreck
reports as we have here."

" Very like," said the brother-in-law. And he
went on with his story. " The ' Thomas Hyke '
was a small iron steamer of six hundred tons,
and she sailed from Ulford for Valparaiso with a
cargo principally of pig-iron."

" Pig-iron for Valparaiso?" remarked the Shipwreck Clerk. And then he knitted his brows
thoughtfully, and said, " Go on."

" She was a new vessel," continued the narrator, " and built with water-tight compartments;
rather uncommon for a vessel of her class, but so
she was. I am not a sailor, and don't know
anything about ships. I went as passenger, and
there was another one named William Anderson,
and his son Sam, a boy about fifteen years old.
We were all going to Valparaiso on business. I
don't remember just how many days we were out,
nor do I know just where we were, but it was
somewhere off the coast of South America, when,
one dark night—with a fog besides, for aught I
know, for I was asleep—we ran into a steamer
coming north. How we managed to do this,

with room enough on both sides for all the ships
in the world to pass, I don't know; but so it was.
When I got on deck the other vessel had gone on,
and we never saw anything more of her. Whether
she sunk or got home is something I can't tell.
But we pretty soon found that the 'Thomas
Hyke' had some of the plates in her bow badly
smashed, and she took in water like a thirsty dog.
The captain had the forward water-tight bulkhead
shut tight, and the pumps set to work, but it was
no use. That forward compartment just filled up
with water, and the 'Thomas Hyke' settled down
with her bow clean under. Her deck was slant-
ing forward like the side of a hill, and the propeller was lifted up so that it wouldn't have
worked even if the engine had been kept going.
The captain had the masts cut away, thinking
this might bring her up some, but it didn't help
much. There was a pretty heavy sea on, and the
waves came rolling up the slant of the deck like
the surf on the sea-shore. The captain gave orders
to have all the hatches battened down so that water
couldn't get in, and the only way by which anybody could go below was by the cabin door, which
was far aft. This work of stopping up all open-
ings in the deck was a dangerous business, for
the decks sloped right down into the water, and
if anybody had slipped, away he'd have gone into
the ocean, with nothing to stop him; but the men
made a line fast to themselves, and worked away

with a good will, and soon got the deck and the
house over the engine as tight as a bottle. The
smoke-stack, which was well forward, had been
broken down by a spar when the masts had been
cut, and as the waves washed into the hole that it
left, the captain had this plugged up with old sails,
well fastened down. It was a dreadful thing to
see the ship a-lying with her bows clean under
water and her stern sticking up. If it hadn't
been for her water-tight compartments that were
left uninjured, she would have gone down to the
bottom as slick as a whistle. On the afternoon
of the day after the collision the wind fell, and
the sea soon became pretty smooth. The captain
was quite sure that there would be no trouble
about keeping afloat until some ship came along
and took us off. Our flag was flying, upside
down, from a pole in the stern; and if anybody
saw a ship making such a guy of herself as the
' Thomas Hyke ' was then doing, they'd be sure
to come to see what was the matter with her,
even if she had no flag of distress flying. We
tried to make ourselves as comfortable as we
could, but this wasn't easy with everything on
such a dreadful slant. But that night we heard
a rumbling and grinding noise down in the hold,
and the slant seemed to get worse. Pretty soon
the captain roused all hands and told us that the
cargo of pig-iron was shifting and sliding down
to the bow, and that it wouldn't be long before

it would break through all the bulkheads, and
then we'd fill and go to the bottom like a shot.
He said we must all take to the boats and get
away as quick as we could. It was an easy
matter launching the boats. They didn't lower
them outside from the davits, but they just let 'em
down on deck and slid 'em along forward into the
water, and then held 'em there with a rope till
everything was ready to start. They launched
three boats, put plenty of provisions and water
in 'em, and then everybody began to get aboard.
But William Anderson and me and his son Sam
couldn't make up our minds to get into those boats
and row out on the dark, wide ocean. They were
the biggest boats we had, but still they were little
things enough. The ship seemed to us to be a
good deal safer, and more likely to be seen when
day broke, than those three boats, which might
be blown off, if the wind rose, nobody knew
where. It seemed to us that the cargo had done
all the shifting it intended to, for the noise below had stopped; and, altogether, we agreed that
we'd rather stick to the ship than go off in those
boats. The captain he tried to make us go, but we
wouldn't do it; and he told us if we chose to stay
behind and be drowned it was our affair and he
couldn't help it; and then he said there was a
small boat aft, and we'd better launch her, and
have her ready in case things should get worse
and we should make up our minds to leave the

vessel. He and the rest then rowed off so as not to be caught in the vortex if the steamer went down, and we three stayed aboard. We launched the small boat in the way we'd seen the others launched, being careful to have ropes tied to us while we were doing it; and we put things aboard that we thought we should want. Then we went into the cabin and waited for morning. It was a queer kind of a cabin, with a floor inclined like the roof of a house; but we sat down in the corners, and were glad to be there. The swinging lamp was burning, and it was a good deal more cheerful in there than it was outside. But, about daybreak, the grinding and rumbling down below began again, and the bow of the ' Thomas Hyke ' kept going down more and more; and it wasn't long before the forward bulkhead of the cabin, which was what you might call its front wall when everything was all right, was under our feet, as level as a floor, and the lamp was lying close against the ceiling that it was hanging from. You may be sure that we thought it was time to get out of that. There were benches with arms to them fastened to the floor, and by these we climbed up to the foot of the cabin stairs, which, being turned bottom upward, we went down in order to get out. When we reached the cabin door we saw part of the deck below us, standing up like the side of a house that is built in the water, as they say the houses in Venice are. We had made our boat fast to the cabin door by a long line, and now we saw her floating quietly on the water, which was very smooth and about twenty feet below us. We drew her up as close under us as we could, and then we let the boy Sam down by a rope, and after some kicking and swinging he got into her; and then he took the oars and kept her right under us while we scrambled down by the ropes which we had used in getting her ready. As soon as we were in the boat we cut her rope and pulled away as hard as we could; and when we got to what we thought was a safe distance we stopped to look at the ' Thomas Hyke.' You never saw such a ship in all your born days. Two thirds of the hull was sunk in the water, and she was standing straight up and down with the stern in the air, her rudder up as high as the topsail ought to be, and the screw propeller looking like the wheel on the top of one of these windmills that they have in the country for pumping up water. Her cargo had shifted so far forward that it had turned her right upon end, but she couldn't sink, owing to the air in the compartments that the water hadn't got into; and on the top of the whole thing was the distress flag flying from the pole which stuck out over the stern. It was broad daylight, but not a thing did we see of the other boats. We'd supposed that they wouldn't row very far, but would lay off at a safe distance until daylight; but they must have been scared and rowed farther than they intended. Well, sir, we stayed in that boat all day and watched the 'Thomas Hyke'; but she just kept as she was and didn't seem to sink an inch. There was no use of rowing away, for we had no place to row to; and besides, we thought that passing ships would be much more likely to see that stern sticking high in the air than our little boat. We had enough to eat, and at night two of us slept while the other watched, dividing off the time and taking turns to this. In the morning there was the 'Thomas Hyke' standing stern up just as before. There was a long swell on the ocean now, and she'd rise and lean over a little on each wave, but she'd come up again just as straight as before. That night passed as the last one had, and in the morning we found we'd drifted a good deal farther from the 'Thomas Hyke'; but she was floating just as she had been, like a big buoy that's moored over a sandbar. We couldn't see a sign of the boats, and we about gave them up. We had our breakfast, which was a pretty poor meal, being nothing but hardtack and what was left of a piece of boiled beef. After we'd sat for a while doing nothing, but feeling mighty uncomfortable, William Anderson said, ' Look here, do you know that I think we would be three fools to keep on shivering all night, and living on hardtack in the daytime, when there's plenty on that vessel for us to eat and to keep us warm. If she's floated that way for two days and two nights, there's no knowing how much longer she'll float, and we might as well go on board and get the things we want as not.' 'All right,' said I, for I was tired doing nothing; and Sam was as willing as anybody. So we rowed up to the steamer, and stopped close to the deck, which, as I said before, was standing straight up out of the water like the wall of a house. The cabin door, which was the only opening into her, was about twenty feet above us, and the ropes which we had tied to the rails of the stairs inside were still hanging down. Sam was an active youngster, and he managed to climb up one of these ropes; but when he got to the door he drew it up and tied knots in it about a foot apart, and then he let it down to us, for neither William Anderson nor me could go up a rope hand over hand without knots or something to hold on to. As it was, we had a lot of bother getting up, but we did it at last; and then we walked up the stairs, treading on the front part of each step instead of the top of it, as we would have done if the stairs had been in their proper position. When we got to the floor of the cabin, which was now perpendicular like a wall, we had to clamber down by means of the furniture, which was screwed fast, until we reached the bulkhead, which was now the floor of the cabin. Close to this bulkhead was a small room which was the steward's pantry, and here we found lots of things to eat, but all jumbled up in a way that made us laugh. The boxes of biscuits and the tin cans and a lot of bottles in wicker covers were piled up on one end of the room, and everything in the lockers and drawers was jumbled together. William Anderson and me set to work to get out what we thought we'd want, and we told Sam to climb up into some of the state-rooms — of which there were four on each side of the cabin — and get some blankets to keep us warm, as well as a few sheets, which we thought we could rig up for an awning to the boat; for the days were just as hot as the nights were cool. When we'd collected what we wanted, William Anderson and me climbed into our own rooms, thinking we'd each pack a valise with what we most wanted to save of our clothes and things; and while we were doing this Sam called out to us that it was raining. He was sitting at the cabin door looking out. I first thought to tell him to shut the door so's to keep the rain from coming in; but when I thought how things really were, I laughed at the idea. There was a sort of little house built over the entrance to the cabin, and in one end of it was the door; and in the way the ship now was the open doorway was underneath the little house, and of course no rain could come in. Pretty soon we heard the rain pouring down, beating on the stern of the vessel like hail. We

got to the stairs and looked out. The rain was
falling in perfect sheets, in a way you never see
except round about the tropics. 'It's a good
thing we're inside,' said William Anderson, 'for
if we'd been out in this rain we'd been drowned
in the boat.' I agreed with him, and we made up
our minds to stay where we were until the rain
was over. Well, it rained about four hours; and
when it stopped, and we looked out, we saw our
little boat nearly full of water, and sunk so deep
that if one of us had stepped on her she'd have
gone down, sure. 'Here's a pretty kittle of fish,'
said William Anderson; 'there's nothing for us
to do now but to stay where we are.' I believe
in his heart he was glad of that, for if ever a man
was tired of a little boat, William Anderson was
tired of that one we'd been in for two days and two
nights. At any rate, there was no use talking
about it, and we set to work to make ourselves
comfortable. We got some mattresses and pillows
out of the state-rooms, and when it began to get
dark we lighted the lamp—which we had filled
with sweet-oil from a flask in the pantry, not
finding any other kind—and we hung it from
the railing of the stairs. We had a good night's
rest, and the only thing that disturbed me was
William Anderson lifting up his head every time
he turned over and saying how much better this
was than that blasted little boat. The next morning we had a good breakfast, even making some

tea with a spirit-lamp we found, using brandy
instead of alcohol. William Anderson and I
wanted to get into the captain's room — which
was near the stern and pretty high up — so as to
see if there was anything there that we ought to
get ready to save when a vessel should come
along and pick us up; but we were not good at
climbing, like Sam, and we didn't see how we
could get up there. Sam said he was sure he
had once seen a ladder in the compartment just
forward of the bulkhead, and as William was
very anxious to get up to the captain's room, we
let the boy go and look for it. There was a sliding door in the bulkhead under our feet, and we
opened this far enough to let Sam get through;
and he scrambled down like a monkey into the
next compartment, which was light enough, although the lower half of it, which was next to
the engine-room, was under the water-line. Sam
actually found a ladder with hooks at one end of
it, and while he was handing it up to us — which
was very hard to do, for he had to climb up on
all sorts of things — he let it topple over, and the
end with the iron hooks fell against the round
glass of one of the port-holes. The glass was
very thick and strong, but the ladder came down
very heavy and shivered it. As bad luck would
have it, this window was below the water-line,
and the water came rushing in in a big spout.
We chucked blankets down to Sam for him to

stop up the hole, but 'twas of no use; for it was hard for him to get at the window, and when he did the water came in with such force that he couldn't get a blanket into the hole. We were afraid he'd be drowned down there, and told him to come out as quick as he could. He put up the ladder again, and hooked it on to the door in the bulkhead, and we held it while he climbed up. Looking down through the doorway, we saw, by the way the water was pouring in at the opening, that it wouldn't be long before that compartment was filled up; so we shoved the door to and made it all tight, and then said William Anderson, ' The ship'll sink deeper and deeper as that fills up, and the water may get up to the cabin door, and we must go and make that as tight as we can.' Sam had pulled the ladder up after him, and this we found of great use in getting to the foot of the cabin stairs. We shut the cabin door, and locked and bolted it; and as it fitted pretty tight, we didn't think it would let in much water if the ship sunk that far. But over the top of the cabin stairs were a couple of folding doors, which shut down horizontally when the ship was in its proper position, and which were only used in very bad, cold weather. These we pulled to and fastened tight, thus having a double protection against the water. Well, we didn't get this done any too soon, for the water did come up to the cabin door, and a little trickled in from the outside door and through the cracks in the inner one. But we went to work and stopped these up with strips from the sheets, which we crammed well in with our pocket-knives. Then we sat down on the steps and waited to see what would happen next. The doors of all the state-rooms were open, and we could see through the thick plate-glass windows in them, which were all shut tight, that the ship was sinking more and more as the water came in. Sam climbed up into one of the after state-rooms, and said the outside water was nearly up to the stern; and pretty soon we looked up to the two port-holes in the stern, and saw that they were covered with water; and as more and more water could be seen there, and as the light came through less easily, we knew that we were sinking under the surface of the ocean. 'It's a mighty good thing,' said William Anderson, 'that no water can get in here.' William had a hopeful kind of mind, and always looked on the bright side of things; but I must say that I was dreadfully scared when I looked through those stern windows and saw water instead of sky. It began to get duskier and duskier as we sank lower and lower; but still we could see pretty well, for it's astonishing how much light comes down through water. After a little while we noticed that the light remained about the same; and then William Anderson he sings out, 'Hooray, we've stopped sinking!' 'What difference does that make?' says I.

' We must be thirty or forty feet under water, and
more yet, for aught I know.' ' Yes, that may be,'
said he ; ' but it is clear that all the water has got
into that compartment that can get in, and we
have sunk just as far down as we are going.'
' But that don't help matters,' said I ; ' thirty or
forty feet under water is just as bad as a thousand
as to drowning a man.' ' Drowning! ' said William ; ' how are you going to be drowned? No
water can get in here.' ' Nor no air, either,'
said I ; ' and people are drowned for want of air,
as I take it.' ' It would be a queer sort of thing,'
said William, ' to be drowned in the ocean and
yet stay as dry as a chip. But it's no use being
worried about air. We've got air enough here to
last us for ever so long. This stern compartment
is the biggest in the ship, and it's got lots of air
in it. Just think of that hold! It must be nearly
full of air. The stern compartment of the hold
has got nothing in it but sewing-machines. I
saw 'em loading her. The pig-iron was mostly
amidships, or at least forward of this compartment. Now, there's no kind of a cargo that'll
accommodate as much air as sewing-machines.
They're packed in wooden frames, not boxes,
and don't fill up half the room they take. There's
air all through and around 'em. It's a very comforting thing to think the hold isn't filled up solid
with bales of cotton or wheat in bulk.' It might
be comforting, but I couldn't get much good out

of it.   And now Sam, who'd been scrambling all
over the cabin to see how things were going on,
sung out that the water was leaking in a little
again at the cabin door and around some of the
iron frames of the windows. ' It's a lucky thing,'
said William Anderson, ' that we didn't sink any
deeper, or the pressure of the water would have
burst in those heavy glasses.   And what we've
got to do now is to stop up all the cracks.   The
more we work the livelier we'll feel.'   We tore off
more strips of sheets and went all round, stopping
up cracks wherever we found them.   ' It's fortunate,' said William Anderson, ' that Sam found
that ladder, for we would have had hard work
getting to the windows of the stern state-rooms
without it; but by resting it on the bottom step
of the stairs, which now happens to be the top
one, we can get to any part of the cabin.'   I
couldn't help thinking that if Sam hadn't found
the ladder it would have been a good deal better
for us; but I didn't want to damp William's
spirits, and I said nothing.

" And now I beg your pardon, sir," said the
narrator, addressing the Shipwreck Clerk, " but
I forgot that you said you'd finish this story yourself. Perhaps you'd like to take it up just here? "

The Shipwreck Clerk seemed surprised, and
had apparently forgotten his previous offer. " Oh
no," said he, " tell your own story.   This is not
a matter of business."

" Very well, then," said the brother-in-law of
J. George Watts, " I'll go on. We made everything as tight as we could, and then we got our
supper, having forgotten all about dinner, and
being very hungry. We didn't make any tea and
we didn't light the lamp, for we knew that would
use up air; but we made a better meal than three
people sunk out of sight in the ocean had a right
to expect. ' What troubles me most,' said William
Anderson, as he turned in, ' is the fact that if we
are forty feet under water our flagpole must be
covered up. Now, if the flag was sticking out,
upside down, a ship sailing by would see it and
would know there was something wrong.' ' If
that's all that troubles you,' said I, ' I guess
you'll sleep easy. And if a ship was to see the
flag, I wonder how they'd know we were down
here, and how they'd get us out if they did! '
' Oh, they'd manage it,' said William Anderson;
' trust those sea-captains for that.' And then he
went to sleep. The next morning the air began
to get mighty disagreeable in the part of the cabin
where we were, and then William Anderson he
says, ' What we've got to do is to climb up into
the stern state-rooms, where the air is purer.
We can come down here to get our meals, and
then go up again to breathe comfortable.' ' And
what are we going to do when the air up there
gets foul? ' says I to William, who seemed to be
making arrangements for spending the summer

in our present quarters. ' Oh, that'll be all right,' said he. ' It don't do to be extravagant with air any more than with anything else. When we've used up all there is in this cabin, we can bore holes through the floor into the hold and let in air from there. If we're economical, there'll be enough to last for dear knows how long.' We passed the night each in a state-room, sleeping on the end wall instead of the berth, and it wasn't till the afternoon of the next day that the air of the cabin got so bad we thought we'd have some fresh; so we went down on the bulkhead, and with an auger that we found in the pantry we bored three holes, about a yard apart, in the cabin floor, which was now one of the walls of the room, just as the bulkhead was the floor, and the stern end, where the two round windows were, was the ceiling or roof. We each took a hole, and I tell you it was pleasant to breathe the air which came in from the hold. ' Isn't this jolly? ' said William Anderson. ' And we ought to be mighty glad that that hold wasn't loaded with codfish or soap. But there's nothing that smells better than new sewing-machines that haven't ever been used, and this air is pleasant enough for anybody.' By William's advice we made three plugs, by which we stopped up the holes when we thought we'd had air enough for the present. ' And now,' says he, ' we needn't climb up into those awkward state-rooms any more. We can just stay down here and be comfortable, and let in air when we want it.' 'And how long do you suppose that air in the hold is going to last?' said I. 'Oh, ever so long,' said he, 'using it so economically as we do; and when it stops coming out lively through these little holes, as I suppose it will after a while, we can saw a big hole in this flooring and go into the hold and do our breathing, if we want to.' That evening we did saw a hole about a foot square, so as to have plenty of air while we were asleep; but we didn't go into the hold, it being pretty well filled up with machines; though the next day Sam and I sometimes stuck our heads in for a good sniff of air, though William Anderson was opposed to this, being of the opinion that we ought to put ourselves on short rations of breathing so as to make the supply of air hold out as long as possible. 'But what's the good,' said I to William, 'of trying to make the air hold out if we've got to be suffocated in this place after all?' 'What's the good?' says he. 'Haven't you enough biscuits and canned meats and plenty of other things to eat, and a barrel of water in that room opposite the pantry, not to speak of wine and brandy if you want to cheer yourself up a bit, and haven't we good mattresses to sleep on, and why shouldn't we try to live and be comfortable as long as we can?' 'What I want,' said I, 'is to get out of this box. The idea of being shut up in here down under the

water is more than I can stand. I'd rather take
my chances going up to the surface and swimming
about till I found a piece of the wreck, or something to float on.' ' You needn't think of anything of that sort,' said William, ' for if we were
to open a door or a window to get out, the
water'd rush in and drive us back and fill up this
place in no time; and then the whole concern
would go to the bottom. And what would you
do if you did get to the top of the water? It's
not likely you'd find anything there to get on,
and if you did you wouldn't live very long floating
about with nothing to eat. No, sir,' says he,
' what we've got to do is to be content with the
comforts we have around us, and something will
turn up to get us out of this; you see if it don't.'
There was no use talking against William Anderson, and I didn't say any more about getting out.
As for Sam, he spent his time at the windows of
the state-rooms a-looking out. We could see a
good way into the water — farther than you would
think — and we sometimes saw fishes, especially
porpoises, swimming about, most likely trying to
find out what a ship was doing hanging bows down
under the water. What troubled Sam was that a
swordfish might come along and jab his sword
through one of the windows. In that case it
would be all up, or rather down, with us.
Every now and then he'd sing out, ' Here comes
one! ' And then, just as I'd give a jump, he'd

say, 'No, it isn't; it's a porpoise.' I thought
from the first, and I think now, that it would have
been a great deal better for us if that boy hadn't
been along. That night there was a good deal of
motion to the ship, and she swung about and rose
up and down more than she had done since we'd
been left in her. 'There must be a big sea running on top,' said William Anderson, 'and if we
were up there we'd be tossed about dreadful.
Now the motion down here is just as easy as a
cradle; and, what's more, we can't be sunk very
deep, for if we were there wouldn't be any motion
at all.' About noon the next day we felt a sudden
tremble and shake run through the whole ship,
and far down under us we heard a rumbling and
grinding that nearly scared me out of my wits. I
first thought we'd struck bottom; but William he
said that couldn't be, for it was just as light in
the cabin as it had been, and if we'd gone down
it would have grown much darker, of course.
The rumbling stopped after a little while, and
then it seemed to grow lighter instead of darker;
and Sam, who was looking up at the stern windows over our heads, he sung out, 'Sky!' And,
sure enough, we could see the blue sky, as clear
as daylight, through those windows! And then
the ship she turned herself on the slant, pretty
much as she had been when her forward compartment first took in water, and we found ourselves
standing on the cabin floor intead of the bulkhead.

I was near one of the open state-rooms, and as I
looked in there was the sunlight coming through
the wet glass in the window, and more cheerful
than anything I ever saw before in this world.
William Anderson he just made one jump, and,
unscrewing one of the state-room windows, he
jerked it open.   We had thought the air inside
was good enough to last some time longer; but
when that window was open and the fresh air
came rushing in, it was a different sort of thing,
I can tell you.   William put his head out and
looked up and down and all around. ‘ She’s
nearly all out of water,’ he shouted, ‘ and we can
open the cabin door!’   Then we all three rushed
at those stairs, which were nearly right side up
now, and we had the cabin doors open in no
time.   When we looked out we saw that the
ship was truly floating pretty much as she had
been when the captain and crew left her, though
we all agreed that her deck didn’t slant as much
forward as it did then.   ‘ Do you know what’s
happened?’ sung out William Anderson, after
he’d stood still for a minute to look around and
think. ‘ That bobbing up and down that the
vessel got last night shook up and settled down
the pig-iron inside of her, and the iron plates in
the bow, that were smashed and loosened by the
collision, have given way under the weight, and
the whole cargo of pig-iron has burst through
and gone to the bottom.   Then, of course, up we

came. Didn't I tell you something would happen to make us all right?'

"Well, I won't make this story any longer than I can help. The next day after that we were taken off by a sugar-ship bound north, and we were carried safe back to Ulford, where we found our captain and the crew, who had been picked up by a ship after they'd been three or four days in their boats. This ship had sailed our way to find us, which, of course, she couldn't do, as at that time we were under water and out of sight.

"And now, sir," said the brother-in-law of J. George Watts to the Shipwreck Clerk, "to which of your classes does this wreck of mine belong?"

"Gents," said the Shipwreck Clerk, rising from his seat, "it's four o'clock, and at that hour this office closes."

OLD PIPES AND THE DRYAD

OLD PIPES AND THE DRYAD

A MOUNTAIN brook ran through a little village. Over the brook there was a narrow bridge, and from the bridge a foot-path led out from the village and up the hillside to the cottage of Old Pipes and his mother. For many, many years Old Pipes had been employed by the villagers to pipe the cattle down from the hills. Every afternoon, an hour before sunset, he would sit on a rock in front of his cottage and play on his pipes. Then all the flocks and herds that were grazing on the mountains would hear him, wherever they might happen to be, and would come down to the village—the cows by the easiest paths, the sheep by those not quite so easy, and the goats by the steep and rocky ways that were hardest of all.

But now, for a year or more, Old Pipes had not piped the cattle home. It is true that every afternoon he sat upon the rock and played upon his

familiar instrument; but the cattle did not hear
him.   He had grown old and his breath was
feeble.   The echoes of his cheerful notes, which
used to come from the rocky hill on the other
side of the valley, were heard no more; and
twenty yards from Old Pipes one could scarcely
tell what tune he was playing.   He had become
somewhat deaf, and did not know that the sound
of his pipes was so thin and weak, and that the
cattle did not hear him.   The cows, the sheep,
and the goats came down every afternoon as before, but this was because two boys and a girl
were sent up after them.   The villagers did not
wish the good old man to know that his piping
was no longer of any use, so they paid him his
little salary every month, and said nothing about
the two boys and the girl.

Old Pipes's mother was, of course, a great deal
older than he was, and was as deaf as a gate—
posts, latch, hinges, and all — and she never knew
that the sound of her son's pipe did not spread
over all the mountain-side and echo back strong
and clear from the opposite hills.   She was very
fond of Old Pipes, and proud of his piping; and
as he was so much younger than she was, she
never thought of him as being very old.   She
cooked for him, and made his bed, and mended
his clothes; and they lived very comfortably on
his little salary.

One afternoon, at the end of the month, when

Old Pipes had finished his piping, he took his stout staff and went down the hill to the village to receive the money for his month's work. The path seemed a great deal steeper and more difficult than it used to be; and Old Pipes thought that it must have been washed by the rains and greatly damaged. He remembered it as a path that was quite easy to traverse either up or down. But Old Pipes had been a very active man, and as his mother was so much older than he was, he never thought of himself as aged and infirm.

When the Chief Villager had paid him, and he had talked a little with some of his friends, Old Pipes started to go home. But when he had crossed the bridge over the brook and gone a short distance up the hillside, he became very tired and sat down upon a stone. He had not been sitting there half a minute when along came two boys and a girl.

"Children," said Old Pipes, "I'm very tired to-night, and I don't believe I can climb up this steep path to my home. I think I shall have to ask you to help me."

"We will do that," said the boys and the girl, quite cheerfully; and one boy took him by the right hand and the other by the left, while the girl pushed him in the back. In this way he went up the hill quite easily, and soon reached his cottage door. Old Pipes gave each of the three children a copper coin, and then they sat down for a few minutes' rest before starting back to the village.

" I'm sorry that I tired you so much," said Old Pipes.

" Oh, that would not have tired us," said one of the boys, " if we had not been so far to-day after the cows, the sheep, and the goats. They rambled high up on the mountain, and we never before had such a time in finding them."

" Had to go after the cows, the sheep, and the goats! " exclaimed Old Pipes. " What do you mean by that? "

The girl, who stood behind the old man, shook her head, put her hand on her mouth, and made all sorts of signs to the boy to stop talking on this subject; but he did not notice her and promptly answered Old Pipes.

" Why, you see, good sir," said he, " that as the cattle can't hear your pipes now, somebody has to go after them every evening to drive them down from the mountain, and the Chief Villager has hired us three to do it. Generally it is not very hard work, but to-night the cattle had wandered far."

" How long have you been doing this? " asked the old man.

The girl shook her head and clapped her hand on her mouth more vigorously than before, but the boy went on.

" I think it is about a year now," he said, " since

the people first felt sure that the cattle could not hear your pipes; and from that time we've been driving them down. But we are rested now and will go home. Good-night, sir."

The three children then went down the hill, the girl scolding the boy all the way home. Old Pipes stood silent a few moments and then he went into his cottage.

" Mother," he shouted, " did you hear what those children said?"

" Children!" exclaimed the old woman; " I did not hear them. I did not know there were any children here."

Then Old Pipes told his mother—shouting very loudly to make her hear—how the two boys and the girl had helped him up the hill, and what he had heard about his piping and the cattle.

" They can't hear you?" cried his mother. " Why, what's the matter with the cattle?"

" Ah me!" said Old Pipes, " I don't believe there's anything the matter with the cattle. It must be with me and my pipes that there is something the matter. But one thing is certain: if I do not earn the wages the Chief Villager pays me, I shall not take them. I shall go straight down to the village and give back the money I received to-day."

" Nonsense!" cried his mother. " I'm sure you've piped as well as you could, and no more can be expected. And what are we to do without the money?"

" I don't know," said Old Pipes; "but I'm going down to the village to pay it back."

The sun had now set; but the moon was shining very brightly on the hillside, and Old Pipes could see his way very well. He did not take the same path by which he had gone before, but followed another, which led among the trees upon the hillside, and, though longer, was not so steep.

When he had gone about half-way the old man sat down to rest, leaning his back against a great oak-tree. As he did so he heard a sound like knocking inside the tree, and then a voice distinctly said:

"Let me out! let me out!"

Old Pipes instantly forgot that he was tired, and sprang to his feet. "This must be a Dryad-tree!" he exclaimed. "If it is, I'll let her out."

Old Pipes had never, to his knowledge, seen a Dryad-tree, but he knew there were such trees on the hillsides and the mountains, and that Dryads lived in them. He knew, too, that in the summer-time, on those days when the moon rose before the sun went down, a Dryad could come out of her tree if any one could find the key which locked her in, and turn it. Old Pipes closely examined the trunk of the tree, which stood in the full moonlight. "If I see that key," he said, "I shall surely turn it." Before long he perceived a piece of bark standing out from the tree, which appeared to him very much like the handle of a key. He took hold of it, and found he could turn it quite around. As he did so a large part of the side of the tree was pushed open, and a beautiful Dryad stepped quickly out.

For a moment she stood motionless, gazing on the scene before her — the tranquil valley, the hills, the forest, and the mountain-side, all lying in the soft clear light of the moon. "Oh, lovely! lovely!" she exclaimed. "How long it is since I have seen anything like this!" And then, turning to Old Pipes, she said, "How good of you to let me out! I am so happy and so thankful that I must kiss you, you dear old man!" And she threw her arms around the neck of Old Pipes and kissed him on both cheeks. "You don't know," she then went on to say, "how doleful it is to be shut up so long in a tree. I don't mind it in the winter, for then I am glad to be sheltered; but in summer it is a rueful thing not to be able to see all the beauties of the world. And it's ever so long since I've been let out. People so seldom come this way; and when they do come at the right time they either don't hear me, or they are frightened and run away. But you, you dear old man, you were not frightened, and you looked and looked for the key, and you let me out, and now I shall not have to go back till winter has come and the air grows cold. Oh, it is glorious!

What can I do for you to show you how grateful
I am?"

"I am very glad," said Old Pipes, "that I let
you out, since I see that it makes you so happy;
but I must admit that I tried to find the key because I had a great desire to see a Dryad. But
if you wish to do something for me, you can,
if you happen to be going down toward the
village."

"To the village!" exclaimed the Dryad. "I
will go anywhere for you, my kind old bene-
factor."

"Well, then," said Old Pipes, "I wish you
would take this little bag of money to the Chief
Villager and tell him that Old Pipes cannot receive pay for the services which he does not perform. It is now more than a year that I have not
been able to make the cattle hear me when I piped
to call them home. I did not know this until to-
night; but now that I know it I cannot keep the
money, and so I send it back." And, handing
the little bag to the Dryad, he bade her good-night
and turned toward his cottage.

"Good-night," said the Dryad. "And I
thank you over and over and over again, you
good old man!"

Old Pipes walked toward his home, very glad
to be saved the fatigue of going all the way down
to the village and back again. "To be sure,"
he said to himself, "this path does not seem at

all steep, and I can walk along it very easily; but it would have tired me dreadfully to come up all the way from the village, especially as I could not have expected those children to help me again." When he reached home his mother was surprised to see him returning so soon.

"What!" she exclaimed, "have you already come back? What did the Chief Villager say? Did he take the money?"

Old Pipes was just about to tell her that he had sent the money to the village by a Dryad when he suddenly reflected that his mother would be sure to disapprove such a proceeding, and so he merely said he had sent it by a person whom he had met.

"And how do you know that the person will ever take it to the Chief Villager?" cried his mother. "You will lose it, and the villagers will never get it. Oh, Pipes! Pipes! when will you be old enough to have ordinary common sense?"

Old Pipes considered that as he was already seventy years of age he could scarcely expect to grow any wiser, but he made no remark on this subject; and, saying that he doubted not that the money would go safely to its destination, he sat down to his supper. His mother scolded him roundly, but he did not mind it; and after supper he went out and sat on a rustic chair in front of the cottage to look at the moon-lit village, and to wonder whether or not the Chief Villager really received the money. While he was doing these two things he went fast asleep.

When Old Pipes left the Dryad, she did not go down to the village with the little bag of money. She held it in her hand and thought about what she had heard. "This is a good and honest old man," she said, "and it is a shame that he should lose this money. He looked as if he needed it, and I don't believe the people in the village will take it from one who has served them so long. Often, when in my tree, have I heard the sweet notes of his pipes. I am going to take the money back to him." She did not start immediately, because there were so many beautiful things to look at; but after a while she went up to the cottage, and, finding Old Pipes asleep in his chair, she slipped the little bag into his coat pocket and silently sped away.

The next day Old Pipes told his mother that he would go up the mountain and cut some wood. He had a right to get wood from the mountain, but for a long time he had been content to pick up the dead branches which lay about his cottage. To-day, however, he felt so strong and vigorous that he thought he would go and cut some fuel that would be better than this. He worked all the morning, and when he came back he did not feel at all tired, and he had a very good appetite for his dinner.

Now, Old Pipes knew a good deal about

Dryads, but there was one thing which, although he had heard, he had forgotten. This was that a kiss from a Dryad made a person ten years younger. The people of the village knew this, and they were very careful not to let any child of ten years or younger go into the woods where the Dryads were supposed to be; for if they should chance to be kissed by one of these tree-nymphs, they would be set back so far that they would cease to exist. A story was told in the village that a very bad boy of eleven once ran away into the woods and had an adventure of this kind; and when his mother found him he was a little baby of one year old. Taking advantage of her opportunity, she brought him up more carefully than she had done before; and he grew to be a very good boy indeed.

Now, Old Pipes had been kissed twice by the Dryad, once on each cheek, and he therefore felt as vigorous and active as when he was a hale man of fifty. His mother noticed how much work he was doing, and told him that he need not try in that way to make up for the loss of his piping wages; for he would only tire himself out and get sick. But her son answered that he had not felt so well for years, and that he was quite able to work. In the course of the afternoon, Old Pipes, for the first time that day, put his hand in his coat pocket, and there, to his amazement, he found the little bag of money. " Well, well! "

he exclaimed, "I am stupid indeed! I really thought that I had seen a Dryad; but when I sat down by that big oak-tree I must have gone to sleep and dreamed it all; and then I came home thinking I had given the money to a Dryad, when it was in my pocket all the time. But the Chief Villager shall have the money. I shall not take it to him to-day; but to-morrow I wish to go to the village to see some of my old friends, and then I shall give up the money."

Toward the close of the afternoon, Old Pipes, as had been his custom for so many years, took his pipes from the shelf on which they lay, and went out to the rock in front of the cottage.

" What are you going to do? " cried his mother. " If you will not consent to be paid, why do you pipe? "

" I am going to pipe for my own pleasure," said her son. " I am used to it, and I do not wish to give it up. It does not matter now whether the cattle hear me or not, and I am sure that my piping will injure no one."

When the good man began to play upon his favorite instrument he was astonished at the sound that came from it. The beautiful notes of the pipes sounded clear and strong down into the valley, and spread over the hills and up the sides of the mountain beyond, while, after a little interval, an echo came back from the rocky hill on the other side of the valley.

"Ha! ha!" he cried, "what has happened to my pipes? They must have been stopped up of late, but now they are as clear and good as ever."

Again the merry notes went sounding far and wide. The cattle on the mountain heard them, and those that were old enough remembered how these notes had called them from their pastures every evening, and so they started down the mountain-side, the others following.

The merry notes were heard in the village below, and the people were much astonished thereby. "Why, who can be blowing the pipes of Old Pipes?" they said. But, as they were all very busy, no one went up to see. One thing, however, was plain enough: the cattle were coming down the mountain. And so the two boys and the girl did not have to go after them, and had an hour for play, for which they were very glad.

The next morning Old Pipes started down to the village with his money, and on the way he met the Dryad. "Oh, ho!" he cried, "is that you? Why, I thought my letting you out of the tree was nothing but a dream."

"A dream!" cried the Dryad; "if you only knew how happy you have made me you would not think it merely a dream. And has it not benefited you? Do you not feel happier? Yesterday I heard you playing beautifully on your pipes."

"Yes, yes," cried he. "I did not understand it before, but I see it all now. I have really grown younger. I thank you, I thank you, good Dryad, from the bottom of my heart. It was the finding of the money in my pocket that made me think it was a dream."

"Oh, I put it in when you were asleep," she said, laughing, "because I thought you ought to keep it. Good-by, kind, honest man. May you live long and be as happy as I am now."

Old Pipes was greatly delighted when he understood that he was really a younger man; but that made no difference about the money, and he kept on his way to the village. As soon as he reached it he was eagerly questioned as to who had been playing his pipes the evening before; and when the people heard that it was himself, they were very much surprised. Thereupon Old Pipes told what had happened to him, and then there was greater wonder, with hearty congratulations and hand-shakes; for Old Pipes was liked by every one. The Chief Villager refused to take his money, and, although Old Pipes said that he had not earned it, every one present insisted that, as he would now play on his pipes as before, he should lose nothing because, for a time, he was unable to perform his duty.

So Old Pipes was obliged to keep his money, and after an hour or two spent in conversation with his friends, he returned to his cottage.

There was one individual, however, who was not at all pleased with what had happened to Old Pipes. This was an Echo-dwarf, who lived on the hills on the other side of the valley, and whose duty it was to echo back the notes of the pipes whenever they could be heard. There were a great many other Echo-dwarfs on these hills, some of whom echoed back the songs of maidens, some the shouts of children, and others the music that was often heard in the village. But there was only one who could send back the strong notes of the pipes of Old Pipes, and this had been his sole duty for many years. But when the old man grew feeble, and the notes of his pipes could not be heard on the opposite hills, this Echo-dwarf had nothing to do, and he spent his time in delightful idleness ; and he slept so much and grew so fat that it made his companions laugh to see him walk.

On the afternoon on which, after so long an interval, the sound of the pipes was heard on the echo-hills, this dwarf was fast asleep behind a rock. As soon as the first notes reached them, some of his companions ran to wake him. Rolling to his feet, he echoed back the merry tune of Old Pipes. Naturally he was very much annoyed and indignant at being thus obliged to give up his life of comfortable leisure, and he hoped very much that this pipe-playing would not occur again. The next afternoon he was awake and listening, and, sure enough, at the usual

hour, along came the notes of the pipes as clear
and strong as they ever had been; and he was
obliged to work as long as Old Pipes played.
The Echo-dwarf was very angry. He had supposed, of course, that the pipe-playing had ceased
forever, and he felt that he had a right to be indignant at being thus deceived. He was so much
disturbed that he made up his mind to go and try
to find out whether this was to be a temporary
matter or not. He had plenty of time, as the
pipes were played but once a day, and he set off
early in the morning for the hill on which Old
Pipes lived. It was hard work for the fat little
fellow, and when he had crossed the valley and
had gone some distance into the woods on the
hillside, he stopped to rest, and in a few minutes
the Dryad came tripping along.

" Ho, ho! " exclaimed the dwarf; " what are
you doing here? and how did you get out of your
tree? "

" Doing! " cried the Dryad, " I am being
happy; that's what I am doing. And I was let
out of my tree by a good old man who plays the
pipes to call the cattle down from the mountain.
And it makes me happier to think that I have
been of service to him. I gave him two kisses of
gratitude, and now he is young enough to play
his pipes as well as ever."

The Echo-dwarf stepped forward, his face pale
with passion. " Am I to believe," he said, " that

you are the cause of this great evil that has come upon me? and that you are the wicked creature who has again started this old man upon his career of pipe-playing? What have I ever done to you that you should have condemned me for years and years to echo back the notes of those wretched pipes?"

At this the Dryad laughed loudly.

"What a funny little fellow you are!" she said. "Any one would think you had been condemned to toil from morning till night; while what you really have to do is merely to imitate for half an hour every day the merry notes of Old Pipes's piping. Fie upon you, Echo-dwarf! You are lazy and selfish; and that is what is the matter with you. Instead of grumbling at being obliged to do a little wholesome work—which is less, I am sure, than that of any other Echo-dwarf upon the rocky hillside—you should rejoice at the good fortune of the old man who has regained so much of his strength and vigor. Go home and learn to be just and generous; and then, perhaps, you may be happy. Good-by."

"Insolent creature!" shouted the dwarf, as he shook his fat little fist at her. "I'll make you suffer for this. You shall find out what it is to heap injury and insult upon one like me, and to snatch from him the repose that he has earned by long years of toil." And, shaking his head savagely, he hurried back to the rocky hillside.

Every afternoon the merry notes of the pipes of Old Pipes sounded down into the valley and over the hills and up the mountain-side; and every afternoon when he had echoed them back, the little dwarf grew more and more angry with the Dryad. Each day, from early morning till it was time for him to go back to his duties upon the rocky hillside, he searched the woods for her. He intended, if he met her, to pretend to be very sorry for what he had said, and he thought he might be able to play a trick upon her which would avenge him well. One day, while thus wandering among the trees, he met Old Pipes. The Echo-dwarf did not generally care to see or speak to ordinary people; but now he was so anxious to find the object of his search that he stopped and asked Old Pipes if he had seen the Dryad. The piper had not noticed the little fellow, and he looked down on him with some surprise.

"No," he said, "I have not seen her, and I have been looking everywhere for her."

"You!" cried the dwarf; "what do you wish with her?"

Old Pipes then sat down on a stone, so that he should be nearer the ear of his small companion, and he told what the Dryad had done for him.

When the Echo-dwarf heard that this was the man whose pipes he was obliged to echo back every day, he would have slain him on the spot had he been able; but, as he was not able, he merely ground his teeth and listened to the rest of the story.

" I am looking for the Dryad now," Old Pipes continued, " on account of my aged mother. When I was old myself, I did not notice how very old my mother was; but now it shocks me to see how feeble and decrepit her years have caused her to become; and I am looking for the Dryad to ask her to make my mother younger, as she made me."

The eyes of the Echo-dwarf glistened. Here was a man who might help him in his plans.

" Your idea is a good one," he said to Old Pipes, " and it does you honor. But you should know that a Dryad can make no person younger but one who lets her out of her tree. However, you can manage the affair very easily. All you need do is to find the Dryad, tell her what you want, and request her to step into her tree and be shut up for a short time. Then you will go and bring your mother to the tree; she will open it, and everything will be as you wish. Is not this a good plan?"

" Excellent! " cried Old Pipes; " and I will go instantly and search more diligently for the Dryad."

" Take me with you," said the Echo-dwarf. " You can easily carry me on your strong shoul-

ders; and I shall be glad to help you in any way
that I can."

"Now, then," said the little fellow to himself,
as Old Pipes carried him rapidly along, "if he
persuades the Dryad to get into a tree—and she
is quite foolish enough to do it—and then goes
away to bring his mother, I shall take a stone or
a club and I will break off the key of that tree,
so that nobody can ever turn it again. Then
Mistress Dryad will see what she has brought
upon herself by her behavior to me."

Before long they came to the great oak-tree in
which the Dryad had lived, and, at a distance,
they saw that beautiful creature herself coming
toward them.

"How excellently well everything happens!"
said the dwarf. "Put me down, and I will go.
Your business with the Dryad is more important
than mine; and you need not say anything about
my having suggested your plan to you. I am
willing that you should have all the credit of it
yourself."

Old Pipes put the Echo-dwarf upon the ground,
but the little rogue did not go away. He con-
cealed himself between some low, mossy rocks,
and he was so much of their color that you would
not have noticed him if you had been looking
straight at him.

When the Dryad came up, Old Pipes lost no
time in telling her about his mother, and what

he wished her to do. At first the Dryad answered nothing, but stood looking very sadly at Old Pipes.

" Do you really wish me to go into my tree again?" she said. " I should dreadfully dislike to do it, for I don't know what might happen. It is not at all necessary, for I could make your mother younger at any time if she would give me the opportunity. I had already thought of making you still happier in this way, and several times I have waited about your cottage, hoping to meet your aged mother; but she never comes outside, and you know a Dryad cannot enter a house. I cannot imagine what put this idea into your head. Did you think of it yourself?"

" No, I cannot say that I did," answered Old Pipes. " A little dwarf whom I met in the woods proposed it to me."

" Oh! " cried the Dryad, " now I see through it all. It is the scheme of that vile Echo-dwarf —your enemy and mine. Where is he? I should like to see him."

" I think he has gone away," said Old Pipes.

" No, he has not," said the Dryad, whose quick eyes perceived the Echo-dwarf among the rocks. " There he is. Seize him and drag him out, I beg of you."

Old Pipes perceived the dwarf as soon as he was pointed out to him, and, running to the rocks, he caught the little fellow by the arm and pulled him out.

"Now, then," cried the Dryad, who had opened the door of the great oak, "just stick him in there and we will shut him up. Then I shall be safe from his mischief for the rest of the time I am free."

Old Pipes thrust the Echo-dwarf into the tree; the Dryad pushed the door shut; there was a clicking sound of bark and wood, and no one would have noticed that the big oak had ever had an opening in it.

"There!" said the Dryad; "now we need not be afraid of him. And I assure you, my good piper, that I shall be very glad to make your mother younger as soon as I can. Will you not ask her to come out and meet me?"

"Of course I will," cried Old Pipes; "and I will do it without delay."

And then, the Dryad by his side, he hurried to his cottage. But when he mentioned the matter to his mother, the old woman became very angry indeed. She did not believe in Dryads; and, if they really did exist, she knew they must be witches and sorceresses, and she would have nothing to do with them. If her son had ever allowed himself to be kissed by one of them, he ought to be ashamed of himself. As to its doing him the least bit of good, she did not believe a word of it. He felt better than he used to feel, but that was very common; she had sometimes felt that way herself. And she forbade him ever to mention a Dryad to her again.

That afternoon Old Pipes, feeling very sad that his plan in regard to his mother had failed, sat down upon the rock and played upon his pipes. The pleasant sounds went down the valley and up the hills and mountain, but, to the great surprise of some persons who happened to notice the fact, the notes were not echoed back from the rocky hillside, but from the woods on the side of the valley on which Old Pipes lived. The next day many of the villagers stopped in their work to listen to the echo of the pipes coming from the woods. The sound was not as clear and strong as it used to be when it was sent back from the rocky hillside, but it certainly came from among the trees. Such a thing as an echo changing its place in this way had never been heard of before, and nobody was able to explain how it could have happened. Old Pipes, however, knew very well that the sound came from the Echo-dwarf shut up in the great oak-tree. The sides of the tree were thin, and the sound of the pipes could be heard through them, and the dwarf was obliged by the laws of his being to echo back those notes whenever they came to him. But Old Pipes thought he might get the Dryad in trouble if he let any one know that the Echo-dwarf was shut up in the tree, and so he wisely said nothing about it.

One day the two boys and the girl who had
helped Old Pipes up the hill were playing in the
woods.   Stopping near the great oak-tree, they
heard a sound of knocking within it, and then a
voice plainly said:

" Let me out! let me out! "

For a moment the children stood still in astonishment, and then one of the boys exclaimed:

" Oh, it is a Dryad, like the one Old Pipes
found!   Let's let her out! "

" What are you thinking of ? " cried the girl.
" I am the oldest of all, and I am only thirteen.
Do you wish to be turned into crawling babies?
Run! run! run! "

And the two boys and the girl dashed down
into the valley as fast as their legs could carry
them.   There was no desire in their youthful
hearts to be made younger than they were.   And
for fear that their parents might think it well that
they should commence their careers anew, they
never said a word about finding the Dryad-tree.

As the summer days went on Old Pipes's
mother grew feebler and feebler.   One day when
her son was away — for he now frequently went
into the woods to hunt or fish, or down into the
valley to work — she arose from her knitting to
prepare the simple dinner.   But she felt so weak
and tired that she was not able to do the work to
which she had been so long accustomed.   " Alas!
alas! " she said, " the time has come when I am

too old to work. My son will have to hire some one to come here and cook his meals, make his bed, and mend his clothes. Alas! alas! I had hoped that as long as I lived I should be able to do these things. But it is not so. I have grown utterly worthless, and some one else must pre- pare the dinner for my son. I wonder where he is." And tottering to the door, she went outside to look for him. She did not feel able to stand, and reaching the rustic chair, she sank into it, quite exhausted, and soon fell asleep.

The Dryad, who had often come to the cottage to see if she could find an opportunity of carrying out Old Pipes's affectionate design, now happened by; and seeing that the much-desired occasion had come, she stepped up quietly behind the old woman and gently kissed her on each cheek, and then as quietly disappeared.

In a few minutes the mother of Old Pipes awoke, and looking up at the sun, she exclaimed, "Why, it is almost dinner-time! My son will be here directly, and I am not ready for him." And rising to her feet, she hurried into the house, made the fire, set the meat and vegetables to cook, laid the cloth, and by the time her son arrived the meal was on the table.

"How a little sleep does refresh one!" she said to herself, as she was bustling about. She was a woman of very vigorous constitution, and at seventy had been a great deal stronger and

more active than her son was at that age.   The
moment Old Pipes saw his mother, he knew that
the Dryad had been there; but, while he felt as
happy as a king, he was too wise to say anything
about her.

" It is astonishing how well I feel to-day," said
his mother; " and either my hearing has improved
or you speak much more plainly than you have
done of late."

The summer days went on and passed away,
the leaves were falling from the trees, and the air
was becoming cold.

" Nature has ceased to be lovely," said the
Dryad, " and the night winds chill me.   It is
time for me to go back into my comfortable
quarters in the great oak.   But first I must pay
another visit to the cottage of Old Pipes."

She found the piper and his mother sitting side
by side on the rock in front of the door.   The
cattle were not to go to the mountain any more
that season, and he was piping them down for
the last time.   Loud and merrily sounded the
pipes of Old Pipes, and down the mountain-side
came the cattle, the cows by the easiest paths,
the sheep by those not quite so easy, and the
goats by the most difficult ones among the rocks;
while from the great oak-tree were heard the
echoes of the cheerful music.

" How happy they look, sitting there together!"
said the Dryad; " and I don't believe it will do ·

them a bit of harm to be still younger." And moving quietly up behind them, she first kissed Old Pipes on his cheek and then his mother.

Old Pipes, who had stopped playing, knew what it was, but he did not move, and said nothing. His mother, thinking that her son had kissed her, turned to him with a smile and kissed him in return. And then she arose and went into the cottage, a vigorous woman of sixty, followed by her son, erect and happy, and twenty years younger than herself.

The Dryad sped away to the woods, shrugging her shoulders as she felt the cool evening wind.

When she reached the great oak, she turned the key and opened the door. "Come out," she said to the Echo-dwarf, who sat blinking within. "Winter is coming on, and I want the comfortable shelter of my tree for myself. The cattle have come down from the mountain for the last time this year, the pipes will no longer sound, and you can go to your rocks and have a holiday until next spring."

Upon hearing these words the dwarf skipped quickly out, and the Dryad entered the tree and pulled the door shut after her. "Now, then," she said to herself, "he can break off the key if he likes. It does not matter to me. Another will grow out next spring. And although the good piper made me no promise, I know that when the warm days arrive next year he will come and let me out again."

The Echo-dwarf did not stop to break the key of the tree. He was too happy to be released to think of anything else, and he hastened as fast as he could to his home on the rocky hillside.

The Dryad was not mistaken when she trusted in the piper. When the warm days came again he went to the oak-tree to let her out. But, to his sorrow and surprise, he found the great tree lying upon the ground. A winter storm had blown it down, and it lay with its trunk shattered and split. And what became of the Dryad no one ever knew.

THE TRANSFERRED GHOST

THE TRANSFERRED GHOST

HE country residence of Mr. John Hinckman was a delightful place to me, for many reasons. It was the abode of a genial, though somewhat impulsive, hospitality. It had broad, smooth-shaven lawns and towering oaks and elms; there were bosky shades at several points, and not far from the house there was a little rill spanned by a rustic bridge with the bark on; there were fruits and flowers, pleasant people, chess, billiards, rides, walks, and fishing. These were great attractions; but none of them, nor all of them together, would have been sufficient to hold me to the place very long. I had been invited for the trout season, but should probably have finished my visit early in the summer had it not been that upon fair days, when the grass was dry, and the sun was not too hot, and there was but little wind, there strolled beneath the lofty elms, or passed lightly through the bosky shades, the form of my Madeline.

This lady was not, in very truth, my Madeline. She had never given herself to me, nor had I, in any way, acquired possession of her. But as I considered her possession the only sufficient reason for the continuance of my existence, I called her, in my reveries, mine. It may have been that I would not have been obliged to confine the use of this possessive pronoun to my reveries had I confessed the state of my feelings to the lady.

But this was an unusually difficult thing to do. Not only did I dread, as almost all lovers dread, taking the step which would in an instant put an end to that delightful season which may be termed the ante-interrogatory period of love, and which might at the same time terminate all intercourse or connection with the object of my passion, but I was also dreadfully afraid of John Hinckman. This gentleman was a good friend of mine, but it would have required a bolder man than I was at that time to ask him for the gift of his niece, who was the head of his household, and, according to his own frequent statement, the main prop of his declining years. Had Madeline acquiesced in my general views on the subject, I might have felt encouraged to open the matter to Mr. Hinckman; but, as I said before, I had never asked her whether or not she would be mine. I thought of these things at all hours of the day and night, particularly the latter.

I was lying awake one night, in the great bed in my spacious chamber, when, by the dim light of the new moon, which partially filled the room, I saw John Hinckman standing by a large chair near the door. I was very much surprised at this, for two reasons. In the first place, my host had never before come into my room; and, in the second place, he had gone from home that morning, and had not expected to return for several days. It was for this reason that I had been able that evening to sit much later than usual with Madeline on the moon-lit porch. The figure was certainly that of John Hinckman in his ordinary dress, but there was a vagueness and indistinctness about it which presently assured me that it was a ghost. Had the good old man been murdered? and had his spirit come to tell me of the deed, and to confide to me the protection of his dear —? My heart fluttered at what I was about to think, but at this instant the figure spoke.

"Do you know," he said, with a countenance that indicated anxiety, "if Mr. Hinckman will return to-night?"

I thought it well to maintain a calm exterior, and I answered:

"We do not expect him."

"I am glad of that," said he, sinking into the

chair by which he stood. " During the two years
and a half that I have inhabited this house, that
man has never before been away for a single
night. You can't imagine the relief it gives me."

And as he spoke he stretched out his legs and
leaned back in the chair. His form became less
vague, and the colors of his garments more distinct and evident, while an expression of gratified
relief succeeded to the anxiety of his countenance.

" Two years and a half! " I exclaimed. " I
don't understand you."

" It is fully that length of time," said the
ghost, " since I first came here. Mine is not an
ordinary case. But before I say anything more
about it, let me ask you again if you are sure Mr.
Hinckman will not return to-night ? "

" I am as sure of it as I can be of anything,"
I answered. " He left to-day for Bristol, two
hundred miles away."

" Then I will go on," said the ghost, " for I
am glad to have the opportunity of talking to
some one who will listen to me; but if John
Hinckman should come in and catch me here I
should be frightened out of my wits."

" This is all very strange," I said, greatly
puzzled by what I had heard. " Are you the
ghost of Mr. Hinckman? "

This was a bold question, but my mind was so
full of other emotions that there seemed to be no
room for that of fear.

" Yes, I am his ghost," my companion replied, " and yet I have no right to be. And this is what makes me so uneasy, and so much afraid of him. It is a strange story, and, I truly believe, without precedent. Two years and a half ago John Hinckman was dangerously ill in this very room. At one time he was so far gone that he was really believed to be dead. It was in consequence of too precipitate a report in regard to this matter that I was, at that time, appointed to be his ghost. Imagine my surprise and horror, sir, when, after I had accepted the position and assumed its responsibilities, that old man revived, became convalescent, and eventually regained his usual health. My situation was now one of extreme delicacy and embarrassment. I had no power to return to my original unembodiment, and I had no right to be the ghost of a man who was not dead. I was advised by my friends to quietly maintain my position, and was assured that, as John Hinckman was an elderly man, it could not be long before I could rightfully assume the position for which I had been selected. But I tell you, sir," he continued, with animation, " the old fellow seems as vigorous as ever, and I have no idea how much longer this annoying state of things will continue. I spend my time trying to get out of that old man's way. I must not leave this house, and he seems to follow me everywhere. I tell you, sir, he haunts me."

" That is truly a queer state of things," I remarked. " But why are you afraid of him? He
couldn't hurt you."

" Of course he couldn't," said the ghost. " But·
his very presence is a shock and terror to me.
Imagine, sir, how you would feel if my case were
yours."

I could not imagine such a thing at all. I
simply shuddered.

" And if one must be a wrongful ghost at all,"
the apparition continued, " it would be much
pleasanter to be the ghost of some man other
than John Hinckman. There is in him an iras-
cibility of temper, accompanied by a facility of
invective, which is seldom met with. And what
would happen if he were to see me, and find out,
as I am sure he would, how long and why I had
inhabited his house, I can scarcely conceive. I
have seen him in his bursts of passion; and, although he did not hurt the people he stormed at
any more than he would hurt me, they seemed to
shrink before him."

All this I knew to be very true. Had it not
been for this peculiarity of Mr. Hinckman I
might have been more willing to talk to him about
his niece.

" I feel sorry for you," I said, for I really began to have a sympathetic feeling toward this unfortunate apparition. " Your case is indeed a hard
one. It reminds me of those persons who have

had doubles, and I suppose a man would often be very angry indeed when he found that there was another being who was personating himself."

" Oh, the cases are not similar at all," said the ghost. " A double or doppelgänger lives on the earth with a man, and, being exactly like him, he makes all sorts of trouble, of course. It is very different with me. I am not here to live with Mr. Hinckman. I am here to take his place. Now, it would make John Hinckman very angry if he knew that. Don't you know it would? "

I assented promptly.

" Now that he is away I can be easy for a little while," continued the ghost; " and I am so glad to have an opportunity of talking to you. I have frequently come into your room and watched you while you slept, but did not dare to speak to you for fear that if you talked with me Mr. Hinckman would hear you and come into the room to know why you were talking to yourself."

" But would he not hear you? " I asked.

" Oh no! " said the other; " there are times when any one may see me, but no one hears me except the person to whom I address myself."

" But why did you wish to speak to me? " I asked.

" Because," replied the ghost, " I like occasionally to talk to people, and especially to some one like yourself, whose mind is so troubled and perturbed that you are not likely to be frightened by a visit from one of us. But I particularly wanted to ask you to do me a favor. There is every probability, so far as I can see, that John Hinckman will live a long time, and my situation is becoming insupportable. My great object at present is to get myself transferred, and I think that you may, perhaps, be of use to me."

"Transferred!" I exclaimed. "What do you mean by that?"

"What I mean," said the other, "is this: now that I have started on my career I have got to be the ghost of somebody, and I want to be the ghost of a man who is really dead."

"I should think that would be easy enough," I said. "Opportunities must continually occur."

"Not at all! not at all!" said my companion, quickly. "You have no idea what a rush and pressure there is for situations of this kind. Whenever a vacancy occurs, if I may express myself in that way, there are crowds of applications for the ghostship."

"I had no idea that such a state of things existed," I said, becoming quite interested in the matter. "There ought to be some regular system, or order of precedence, by which you could all take your turns like customers in a barber's shop."

"Oh dear, that would never do at all!" said the other. "Some of us would have to wait forever. There is always a great rush whenever a good ghostship offers itself — while, as you know, there are some positions that no one would care for. And it was in consequence of my being in too great a hurry on an occasion of the kind that I got myself into my present disagreeable predicament, and I have thought that it might be possible that you would help me out of it. You might know of a case where an opportunity for a ghostship was not generally expected, but which might present itself at any moment. If you would give me a short notice I know I could arrange for a transfer."

"What do you mean?" I exclaimed. "Do you want me to commit suicide? or to undertake a murder for your benefit?"

"Oh no, no, no!" said the other, with a vapory smile. "I mean nothing of that kind. To be sure, there are lovers who are watched with considerable interest, such persons having been known, in moments of depression, to offer very desirable ghostships; but I did not think of anything of that kind in connection with you. You were the only person I cared to speak to, and I hoped that you might give me some information that would be of use; and, in return, I shall be very glad to help you in your love-affair."

"You seem to know that I have such an affair," I said.

"Oh yes!" replied the other, with a little

yawn. "I could not be here so much as I have been without knowing all about that."

There was something horrible in the idea of Madeline and myself having been watched by a ghost, even, perhaps, when we wandered together in the most delightful and bosky places. But then this was quite an exceptional ghost, and I could not have the objections to him which would ordinarily arise in regard to beings of his class.

"I must go now," said the ghost, rising, "but I will see you somewhere to-morrow night. And remember—you help me and I'll help you."

I had doubts the next morning as to the propriety of telling Madeline anything about this interview, and soon convinced myself that I must keep silent on the subject. If she knew there was a ghost about the house she would probably leave the place instantly. I did not mention the matter, and so regulated my demeanor that I am quite sure Madeline never suspected what had taken place. For some time I had wished that Mr. Hinckman would absent himself, for a day at least, from the premises. In such case I thought I might more easily nerve myself up to the point of speaking to Madeline on the subject of our future collateral existence; and, now that the opportunity for such speech had really occurred, I did not feel ready to avail myself of it. What would become of me if she refused me?

I had an idea, however, that the lady thought that, if I were going to speak at all, this was the time. She must have known that certain sentiments were afloat within me, and she was not unreasonable in her wish to see the matter settled one way or the other. But I did not feel like taking a bold step in the dark. If she wished me to ask her to give herself to me she ought to offer me some reason to suppose that she would make the gift. If I saw no probability of such generosity I would prefer that things should remain as they were.

That evening I was sitting with Madeline in the moon-lit porch. It was nearly ten o'clock, and ever since supper-time I had been working myself up to the point of making an avowal of my sentiments. I had not positively determined to do this, but wished gradually to reach the proper point, when, if the prospect looked bright, I might speak. My companion appeared to understand the situation — at least I imagined that the nearer I came to a proposal the more she seemed to expect it. It was certainly a very critical and important epoch in my life. If I spoke I should make myself happy or miserable forever; and if I did not speak I had every reason to believe that the lady would not give me another chance to do so.

Sitting thus with Madeline, talking a little, and

thinking very hard over these momentous matters, I looked up and saw the ghost not a dozen feet away from us. He was sitting on the railing of the porch, one leg thrown up before him, the other dangling down as he leaned against a post. He was behind Madeline, but almost in front of me, as I sat facing the lady. It was fortunate that Madeline was looking out over the landscape, for I must have appeared very much startled. The ghost had told me that he would see me sometime this night, but I did not think he would make his appearance when I was in the company of Madeline. If she should see the spirit of her uncle I could not answer for the consequences. I made no exclamation, but the ghost evidently saw that I was troubled.

" Don't be afraid," he said. " I shall not let her see me; and she cannot hear me speak unless I address myself to her, which I do not intend to do."

I suppose I looked grateful.

" So you need not trouble yourself about that," the ghost continued; " but it seems to me that you are not getting along very well with your affair. If I were you I should speak out without waiting any longer. You will never have a better chance. You are not likely to be inter-rupted; and, so far as I can judge, the lady seems disposed to listen to you favorably; that is, if she ever intends to do so. There is no

knowing when John Hinckman will go away
again; certainly not this summer.   If I were in
your place I should never dare to make love to
Hinckman's niece if he were anywhere about the
place.   If he should catch any one offering himself to Miss Madeline he would then be a terrible
man to encounter."

I agreed perfectly to all this.

" I cannot bear to think of him! " I ejaculated
aloud.

" Think of whom? " asked Madeline, turning
quickly toward me.

Here was an awkward situation.   The long
speech of the ghost, to which Madeline paid no
attention, but which I heard with perfect distinct-
ness, had made me forget myself.

It was necessary to explain quickly.   Of course
it would not do to admit that it was of her dear
uncle that I was speaking; and so I mentioned
hastily the first name I thought of.

" Mr. Vilars," I said.

This statement was entirely correct; for I
never could bear to think of Mr. Vilars, who was
a gentleman who had at various times paid much
attention to Madeline.

" It is wrong for you to speak in that way of
Mr. Vilars," she said.   " He is a remarkably
well-educated and sensible young man, and has
very pleasant manners.   He expects to be elected
to the legislature this fall, and I should not be

surprised if he made his mark. He will do well in a legislative body, for whenever Mr. Vilars has anything to say he knows just how and when to say it."

This was spoken very quietly and without any show of resentment, which was all very natural; for if Madeline thought at all favorably of me she could not feel displeased that I should have disagreeable emotions in regard to a possible rival. The concluding words contained a hint which I was not slow to understand. I felt very sure that if Mr. Vilars were in my present position he would speak quickly enough.

" I know it is wrong to have such ideas about a person," I said, " but I cannot help it."

The lady did not chide me, and after this she seemed even in a softer mood. As for me, I felt considerably annoyed, for I had not wished to admit that any thought of Mr. Vilars had ever occupied my mind.

" You should not speak aloud that way," said the ghost, " or you may get yourself into trouble. I want to see everything go well with you, because then you may be disposed to help me, especially if I should chance to be of any assistance to you, which I hope I shall be."

I longed to tell him that there was no way in which he could help me so much as by taking his instant departure. To make love to a young lady with a ghost sitting on the railing near by, and that ghost the apparition of a much-dreaded uncle, the very idea of whom in such a position and at such a time made me tremble, was a difficult, if not an impossible, thing to do; but I forbore to speak, although I may have looked, my mind.

" I suppose," continued the ghost, " that you have not heard anything that might be of advantage to me. Of course I am very anxious to hear; but if you have anything to tell me I can wait until you are alone. I will come to you to-night in your room, or I will stay here until the lady goes away."

" You need not wait here," I said; " I have nothing at all to say to you."

Madeline sprang to her feet, her face flushed and her eyes ablaze.

" Wait here! " she cried. " What do you suppose I am waiting for? Nothing to say to me indeed! — I should think so! What should you have to say to me? "

" Madeline," I exclaimed, stepping toward her, " let me explain."

But she had gone.

Here was the end of the world for me! I turned fiercely to the ghost.

" Wretched existence! " I cried. " You have ruined everything. You have blackened my whole life. Had it not been for you—"

But here my voice faltered. I could say no more.

"You wrong me," said the ghost. "I have not injured you. I have tried only to encourage and assist you, and it is your own folly that has done this mischief. But do not despair. Such mistakes as these can be explained. Keep up a brave heart. Good-by."

And he vanished from the railing like a bursting soap-bubble.

I went gloomily to bed, but I saw no apparitions that night except those of despair and misery which my wretched thoughts called up. The words I had uttered had sounded to Madeline like the basest insult. Of course there was only one interpretation she could put upon them.

As to explaining my ejaculations, that was impossible. I thought the matter over and over again as I lay awake that night, and I determined that I would never tell Madeline the facts of the case. It would be better for me to suffer all my life than for her to know that the ghost of her uncle haunted the house. Mr. Hinckman was away, and if she knew of his ghost she could not be made to believe that he was not dead. She might not survive the shock! No, my heart could bleed, but I would never tell her.

The next day was fine, neither too cool nor too warm; the breezes were gentle, and Nature smiled. But there were no walks or rides with Madeline. She seemed to be much engaged during the day, and I saw but little of her.

When we met at meals she was polite, but very quiet and reserved. She had evidently determined on a course of conduct, and had resolved to assume that, although I had been very rude to her, she did not understand the import of my words. It would be quite proper, of course, for her not to know what I meant by my expressions of the night before.

I was downcast and wretched and said but little, and the only bright streak across the black horizon of my woe was the fact that she did not appear to be happy, although she affected an air of unconcern. The moon-lit porch was deserted that evening, but wandering about the house, I found Madeline in the library alone. She was reading, but I went in and sat down near her. I felt that, although I could not do so fully, I must in a measure explain my conduct of the night before. She listened quietly to a somewhat labored apology I made for the words I had used.

" I have not the slightest idea what you meant," she said, " but you were very rude."

I earnestly disclaimed any intention of rudeness, and assured her, with a warmth of speech that must have made some impression upon her, that rudeness to her would be an action impossible to me. I said a great deal upon the subject, and implored her to believe that if it were not for a certain obstacle I could speak to her so plainly that she would understand everything.

She was silent for a time, and then she said, rather more kindly, I thought, than she had spoken before:

" Is that obstacle in any way connected with my uncle? "

" Yes," I answered, after a little hesitation, " it is, in a measure, connected with him."

She made no answer to this, and sat looking at her book, but not reading. From the expression of her face I thought she was somewhat softened toward me. She knew her uncle as well as I did, and she may have been thinking that, if he were the obstacle that prevented my speaking (and there were many ways in which he might be that obstacle), my position would be such a hard one that it would excuse some wildness of speech and eccentricity of manner. I saw, too, that the warmth of my partial explanations had had some effect on her, and I began to believe that it might be a good thing for me to speak my mind without delay. No matter how she should receive my proposition, my relations with her could not be worse than they had been the previous night and day, and there was something in her face which encouraged me to hope that she might forget my foolish exclamations of the evening before if I began to tell her my tale of love.

I drew my chair a little nearer to her, and as I did so the ghost burst into the room from the doorway behind her. I say burst, although no door flew open and he made no noise. He was wildly excited, and waved his arms above his head. The moment I saw him my heart fell within me. With the entrance of that impertinent apparition every hope fled from me. I could not speak while he was in the room.

I must have turned pale; and I gazed steadfastly at the ghost, almost without seeing Madeline, who sat between us.

"Do you know," he cried, "that John Hinckman is coming up the hill? He will be here in fifteen minutes; and if you are doing anything in the way of love-making you had better hurry it up. But this is not what I came to tell you. I have glorious news! At last I am transferred! Not forty minutes ago a Russian nobleman was murdered by the Nihilists. Nobody ever thought of him in connection with an immediate ghostship. My friends instantly applied for the situation for me, and obtained my transfer. I am off before that horrid Hinckman comes up the hill. The moment I reach my new position I shall put off this hated semblance. Good-by. You can't imagine how glad I am to be, at last, the real ghost of somebody."

"Oh!" I cried, rising to my feet, and stretching out my arms in utter wretchedness, "I would to Heaven you were mine!"

"I *am* yours," said Madeline, raising to me her tearful eyes.

"THE PHILOSOPHY OF RELATIVE EXISTENCES"

"THE PHILOSOPHY OF RELA-
TIVE EXISTENCES"

IN a certain summer, not long gone, my friend Bentley and I found ourselves in a little hamlet which overlooked a placid valley, through which a river gently moved, winding its way through green stretches until it turned the end of a line of low hills and was lost to view. Beyond this river, far away, but visible from the door of the cottage where we dwelt, there lay a city. Through the mists which floated over the valley we could see the outlines of steeples and tall roofs; and buildings of a character which indicated thrift and business stretched themselves down to the opposite edge of the river. The more distant parts of the city, evidently a small one, lost themselves in the hazy summer atmosphere.

Bentley was young, fair-haired, and a poet; I was a philosopher, or trying to be one. We

were good friends, and had come down into this
peaceful region to work together. Although we
had fled from the bustle and distractions of the
town, the appearance in this rural region of a city,
which, so far as we could observe, exerted no influence on the quiet character of the valley in
which it lay, aroused our interest. No craft
plied up and down the river; there were no
bridges from shore to shore; there were none of
those scattered and half-squalid habitations which
generally are found on the outskirts of a city;
there came to us no distant sound of bells; and
not the smallest wreath of smoke rose from any
of the buildings.

In answer to our inquiries our landlord told
us that the city over the river had been built by
one man, who was a visionary, and who had a
great deal more money than common sense.
" It is not as big a town as you would think,
sirs," he said, " because the general mistiness of
things in this valley makes them look larger than
they are. Those hills, for instance, when you get
to them are not as high as they look to be from
here. But the town is big enough, and a good
deal too big; for it ruined its builder and owner,
who when he came to die had not money enough
left to put up a decent tombstone at the head of
his grave. He had a queer idea that he would
like to have his town all finished before anybody
lived in it, and so he kept on working and spend-

ing money year after year and year after year
until the city was done and he had not a cent left.
During all the time that the place was building
hundreds of people came to him to buy houses,
or to hire them, but he would not listen to anything of the kind. No one must live in his town
until it was all done. Even his workmen were
obliged to go away at night to lodge. It is a
town, sirs, I am told, in which nobody has slept
for even a night. There are streets there, and
places of business, and churches, and public
halls, and everything that a town full of inhabitants could need; but it is all empty and
deserted, and has been so as far back as I can
remember, and I came to this region when I
was a little boy."

"And is there no one to guard the place?" we
asked; "no one to protect it from wandering
vagrants who might choose to take possession of
the buildings?"

"There are not many vagrants in this part of
the country," he said, "and if there were they
would not go over to that city. It is haunted."

"By what?" we asked.

"Well, sirs, I scarcely can tell you; queer beings that are not flesh and blood, and that is all I
know about it. A good many people living here-
abouts have visited that place once in their lives,
but I know of no one who has gone there a
second time."

" And travellers," I said, " are they not excited by curiosity to explore that strange uninhabited city? "

" Oh yes," our host replied; " almost all visitors to the valley go over to that queer city — generally in small parties, for it is not a place in which one wishes to walk about alone. Sometimes they see things and sometimes they don't. But I never knew any man or woman to show a fancy for living there, although it is a very good town."

This was said at supper-time, and, as it was the period of full moon, Bentley and I decided that we would visit the haunted city that evening. Our host endeavored to dissuade us, saying that no one ever went over there at night; but as we were not to be deterred he told us where we would find his small boat tied to a stake on the river-bank. We soon crossed the river, and landed at a broad but low stone pier, at the land end of which a line of tall grasses waved in the gentle night wind as if they were sentinels warning us from entering the silent city. We pushed through these, and walked up a street fairly wide, and so well paved that we noticed none of the weeds and other growths which generally denote desertion or little use. By the bright light of the moon we could see that the architecture was simple, and of a character highly gratifying to the eye. All the buildings were of stone, and of good size. We were greatly excited and interested, and proposed to continue our walks until the moon should set, and to return on the following morning—"to live here, perhaps," said Bentley. "What could be so romantic and yet so real? What could conduce better to the marriage of verse and philosophy?" But as he said this we saw around the corner of a cross-street some forms as of people hurrying away.

"The spectres," said my companion, laying his hand on my arm.

"Vagrants, more likely," I answered, "who have taken advantage of the superstition of the region to appropriate this comfort and beauty to themselves."

"If that be so," said Bentley, "we must have a care for our lives."

We proceeded cautiously, and soon saw other forms fleeing before us and disappearing, as we supposed, around corners and into houses. And now suddenly finding ourselves upon the edge of a wide, open public square, we saw in the dim light—for a tall steeple obscured the moon—the forms of vehicles, horses, and men moving here and there. But before, in our astonishment, we could say a word one to the other, the moon moved past the steeple, and in its bright light we could see none of the signs of life and traffic which had just astonished us.

Timidly, with hearts beating fast, but with not

one thought of turning back, nor any fear of
vagrants — for we were now sure that what we
had seen was not flesh and blood, and therefore
harmless — we crossed the open space and entered
a street down which the moon shone clearly.
Here and there we saw dim figures, which
quickly disappeared; but, approaching a low
stone balcony in front of one of the houses, we
were surprised to see, sitting thereon and leaning
over a book which lay open upon the top of the
carved parapet, the figure of a woman who did
not appear to notice us.

"That is a real person," whispered Bentley,
"and she does not see us."

"No," I replied; "it is like the others. Let
us go near it."

We drew near to the balcony and stood before
it. At this the figure raised its head and looked
at us. It was beautiful, it was young; but its
substance seemed to be of an ethereal quality
which we had never seen or known of. With
its full, soft eyes fixed upon us, it spoke.

"Why are you here?" it asked. "I have said
to myself that the next time I saw any of you I
would ask you why you come to trouble us.
Cannot you live content in your own realms and
spheres, knowing, as you must know, how timid
we are, and how you frighten us and make us un-
happy? In all this city there is, I believe, not
one of us except myself who does not flee and

hide from you whenever you cruelly come here. Even I would do that, had not I declared to myself that I would see you and speak to you, and endeavor to prevail upon you to leave us in peace."

The clear, frank tones of the speaker gave me courage. "We are two men," I answered, "strangers in this region, and living for the time in the beautiful country on the other side of the river. Having heard of this quiet city, we have come to see it for ourselves. We had supposed it to be uninhabited, but now that we find that this is not the case, we would assure you from our hearts that we do not wish to disturb or annoy any one who lives here. We simply came as honest travellers to view the city."

The figure now seated herself again, and as her countenance was nearer to us, we could see that it was filled with pensive thought. For a moment she looked at us without speaking. "Men!" she said. "And so I have been right. For a long time I have believed that the beings who sometimes come here, filling us with dread and awe, are men."

"And you," I exclaimed—"who are you, and who are these forms that we have seen, these strange inhabitants of this city?"

She gently smiled as she answered, "We are the ghosts of the future. We are the people who are to live in this city generations hence. But all

of us do not know that, principally because we do
not think about it and study about it enough to
know it.   And it is generally believed that the
men and women who sometimes come here are
ghosts who haunt the place."

"And that is why you are terrified and flee
from us?" I exclaimed. "You think we are
ghosts from another world?"

"Yes," she replied; "that is what is thought,
and what I used to think."

"And you," I asked, "are spirits of human
beings yet to be?"

"Yes," she answered; "but not for a long
time.   Generations of men—I know not how
many—must pass away before we are men and
women."

"Heavens!" exclaimed Bentley, clasping his
hands and raising his eyes to the sky, "I shall
be a spirit before you are a woman."

"Perhaps," she said again, with a sweet smile
upon her face, "you may live to be very, very
old."

But Bentley shook his head. This did not
console him.   For some minutes I stood in con-
templation, gazing upon the stone pavement beneath my feet. "And this," I ejaculated, "is a
city inhabited by the ghosts of the future, who
believe men and women to be phantoms and
spectres?"

She bowed her head.

" But how is it," I asked, " that you discovered that you are spirits and we mortal men? "

" There are so few of us who think of such things," she answered, "so few who study, ponder, and reflect. I am fond of study, and I love philosophy; and from the reading of many books I have learned much. From the book which I have here I have learned most; and from its teachings I have gradually come to the belief, which you tell me is the true one, that we are spirits and you men."

" And what book is that? " I asked.

" It is ' The Philosophy of Relative Existences,' by Rupert Vance."

" Ye gods! " I exclaimed, springing upon the balcony, "that is my book, and I am Rupert Vance." I stepped toward the volume to seize it, but she raised her hand.

" You cannot touch it," she said. " It is the ghost of a book. And did you write it? "

" Write it ? No," I said; " I am writing it. It is not yet finished."

" But here it is," she said, turning over the last pages. " As a spirit book it is finished. It is very successful; it is held in high estimation by intelligent thinkers; it is a standard work."

I stood trembling with emotion. " High estimation! " I said. " A standard work! "

" Oh yes," she replied, with animation; " and

it well deserves its great success, especially in its conclusion. I have read it twice."

"But let me see these concluding pages," I exclaimed. "Let me look upon what I am to write."

She smiled, and shook her head, and closed the book. "I would like to do that," she said, "but if you are really a man you must not know what you are going to do."

"Oh, tell me, tell me," cried Bentley from below, "do you know a book called 'Stellar Studies,' by Arthur Bentley? It is a book of poems."

The figure gazed at him. "No," it said, presently, "I never heard of it."

I stood trembling. Had the youthful figure before me been flesh and blood, had the book been a real one, I would have torn it from her.

"O wise and lovely being!" I exclaimed, falling on my knees before her, "be also benign and generous. Let me but see the last page of my book. If I have been of benefit to your world; more than all, if I have been of benefit to you, let me see, I implore you — let me see how it is that I have done it."

She rose with the book in her hand. "You have only to wait until you have done it," she said, "and then you will know all that you could see here." I started to my feet and stood alone upon the balcony.

"I am sorry," said Bentley, as we walked toward the pier where we had left our boat, "that we talked only to that ghost girl, and that the other spirits were all afraid of us. Persons whose souls are choked up with philosophy are not apt to care much for poetry; and even if my book is to be widely known, it is easy to see that she may not have heard of it."

I walked triumphant. The moon, almost touching the horizon, beamed like red gold. "My dear friend," said I, "I have always told you that you should put more philosophy into your poetry. That would make it live."

"And I have always told you," said he, "that you should not put so much poetry into your philosophy. It misleads people."

"It didn't mislead that ghost girl," said I.

"How do you know?" said Bentley. "Perhaps she is wrong, and the other inhabitants of the city are right, and we may be the ghosts after all. Such things, you know, are only relative. Anyway," he continued, after a little pause, "I wish I knew that those ghosts were now reading the poem which I am going to begin to-morrow."

A PIECE OF RED CALICO

A PIECE OF RED CALICO

I WAS going into town one morning from my suburban residence, when my wife handed me a little piece of red calico, and asked me if I would have time, during the day, to buy her two yards and a half of calico like that. I assured her that it would be no trouble at all; and putting the sample in my pocket, I took the train for the city.

At lunch-time I stopped in at a large dry-goods store to attend to my wife's commission. I saw a well-dressed man walking the floor between the counters, where long lines of girls were waiting on much longer lines of customers, and asked him where I could see some red calico.

"This way, sir." And he led me up the store. "Miss Stone," said he to a young lady, "show this gentleman some red calico."

"What shade do you want?" asked Miss Stone.

I showed her the little piece of calico that my wife had given me. She looked at it and handed

it back to me. Then she took down a great roll
of red calico and spread it out on the counter.

" Why, that isn't the shade! " said I.

" No, not exactly," said she ; " but it is prettier
than your sample."

" That may be," said I ; " but, you see, I want
to match this piece. There is something already
made of this kind of calico which needs to be en-
larged or mended or something. I want some
calico of the same shade."

The girl made no answer, but took down another
roll.

" That's the shade," said she.

" Yes," I replied, " but it's striped."

" Stripes are more worn than anything else in
calicoes," said she.

" Yes, but this isn't to be worn. It's for furniture, I-think. At any rate, I want perfectly plain
stuff, to match something already in use."

" Well, I don't think you can find it perfectly
plain unless you get Turkey red."

" What is Turkey red? " I asked.

" Turkey red is perfectly plain in calicoes," she
answered.

" Well, let me see some."

" We haven't any Turkey-red calico left," she
said, " but we have some very nice plain calicoes
in other colors."

" I don't want any other color. I want stuff
to match this."

"It's hard to match cheap calico like that," she said. And so I left her.

I next went into a store a few doors farther up the street. When I entered I approached the "floor-walker," and handing him my sample, said:

"Have you any calico like this?"

"Yes, sir," said he. "Third counter to the right."

I went to the third counter to the right, and showed my sample to the salesman in attendance there. He looked at it on both sides. Then he said:

"We haven't any of this."

"I was told you had," said I.

"We had it, but we're out of it now. You'll get that goods at an upholsterer's."

I went across the street to an upholsterer's.

"Have you any stuff like this?" I asked.

"No," said the salesman, "we haven't. Is it for furniture?"

"Yes," I replied.

"Then Turkey red is what you want."

"Is Turkey red just like this?" I asked.

"No," said he; "but it's much better."

"That makes no difference to me," I replied. "I want something just like this."

"But they don't use that for furniture," he said.

"I should think people could use anything

they wanted for furniture," I remarked, somewhat sharply.

" They can, but they don't," he said, quite
calmly. " They don't use red like that. They
use Turkey red."

I said no more, but left. The next place I
visited was a very large dry-goods store. Of the
first salesman I saw I inquired if they kept red
calico like my sample.

" You'll find that on the second story," said
he.

I went upstairs. There I asked a man :
" Where will I find red calico? "

" In the far room to the left. Over there."
And he pointed to a distant corner.

I walked through the crowds of purchasers and
salespeople, and around the counters and tables
filled with goods, to the far room to the left.
When I got there I asked for red calico.

" The second counter down this side," said the
man.

I went there and produced my sample. " Calicoes downstairs," said the man.

" They told me they were up here," I said.

" Not these plain goods. You'll find 'em
downstairs at the back of the store, over on that
side."

I went downstairs to the back of the store.

" Where will I find red calico like this? " I
asked.

"Next counter but one," said the man addressed, walking with me in the direction pointed out.

"Dunn, show red calicoes."

Mr. Dunn took my sample and looked at it.

"We haven't this shade in that quality of goods," he said.

"Well, have you it in any quality of goods?" I asked.

"Yes; we've got it finer." And he took down a piece of calico, and unrolled a yard or two of it on the counter.

"That's not this shade," I said.

"No," said he. "The goods is finer and the color's better."

"I want it to match this," I said.

"I thought you weren't particular about the match," said the salesman. "You said you didn't care for the quality of the goods, and you know you can't match goods without you take into consideration quality and color both. If you want that quality of goods in red, you ought to get Turkey red."

I did not think it necessary to answer this remark, but said:

"Then you've got nothing to match this?"

"No, sir. But perhaps they may have it in the upholstery department, in the sixth story."

So I got in the elevator and went up to the top of the house.

" Have you any red stuff like this? " I said to a young man.

" Red stuff? Upholstery department—other end of this floor."

I went to the other end of the floor.

" I want some red calico," I said to a man.

" Furniture goods? " he asked.

" Yes," said I.

" Fourth counter to the left."

I went to the fourth counter to the left, and showed my sample to a salesman. He looked at it, and said:

" You'll get this down on the first floor—calico department."

I turned on my heel, descended in the elevator, and went out on the street. I was thoroughly sick of red calico. But I determined to make one more trial. My wife had bought her red calico not long before, and there must be some to be had somewhere. I ought to have asked her where she obtained it, but I thought a simple little thing like that could be bought anywhere.

I went into another large dry-goods store. As I entered the door a sudden tremor seized me. I could not bear to take out that piece of red calico. If I had had any other kind of a rag about me— a pen-wiper or anything of the sort—I think I would have asked them if they could match that.

But I stepped up to a young woman and presented my sample, with the usual question.

" Back room, counter on the left," she said.

I went there.

" Have you any red calico like this?" I asked of the saleswoman behind the counter.

" No, sir," she said, " but we have it in Turkey red."

Turkey red again!   I surrendered.

" All right," I said, " give me Turkey red."

" How much, sir? " she asked.

" I don't know — say five yards."

She looked at me rather strangely, but measured off five yards of Turkey-red calico.   Then she rapped on the counter and called out " Cash! " A little girl, with yellow hair in two long plaits, came slowly up.   The lady wrote the number of yards, the name of the goods, her own number, the price, the amount of the bank-note I handed her, and some other matters, probably the color of my eyes and the direction and velocity of the wind, on a slip of paper.   She then copied all this into a little book which she kept by her. Then she handed the slip of paper, the money, and the Turkey red to the yellow-haired girl. This young person copied the slip into a little book she carried, and then she went away with the calico, the paper slip, and the money.

After a very long time — during which the little girl probably took the goods, the money, and the slip to some central desk, where the note was received, its amount and number entered in a book, change given to the girl, a copy of the slip made and entered, girl's entry examined and approved, goods wrapped up, girl registered, plaits counted and entered on a slip of paper and copied by the girl in her book, girl taken to a hydrant and washed, number of towel entered on a paper slip and copied by the girl in her book, value of my note and amount of change branded somewhere on the child, and said process noted on a slip of paper and copied in her book—the girl came to me, bringing my change and the package of Turkey-red calico.

I had time for but very little work at the office that afternoon, and when I reached home I handed the package of calico to my wife. She unrolled it and exclaimed:

" Why, this don't match the piece I gave you! "

" Match it! " I cried. " Oh no! it don't match it. You didn't want that matched. You were mistaken. What you wanted was Turkey red—third counter to the left. I mean, Turkey red is what they use."

My wife looked at me in amazement, and then I detailed to her my troubles.

" Well," said she, " this Turkey red is a great deal prettier than what I had, and you've got so much of it that I needn't use the other at all. I wish I had thought of Turkey red before."

" I wish from the bottom of my heart you had," said I.

9 783744 704748